Godfrey Higgins

Horae sabbaticae

Or, An Attempt to correct certain superstitious and vulgar Errors

respecting the Sabbath

Godfrey Higgins

Horae sabbaticae
Or, An Attempt to correct certain superstitious and vulgar Errors respecting the Sabbath

ISBN/EAN: 9783337130817

Printed in Europe, USA, Canada, Australia, Japan

Cover: Foto ©ninafisch / pixelio.de

More available books at **www.hansebooks.com**

HORÆ SABBATICÆ;

OR,

AN ATTEMPT TO CORRECT CERTAIN

SUPERSTITIOUS AND VULGAR ERRORS

RESPECTING

THE SABBATH.

BY GODFREY HIGGINS, ESQ.

F. S. A., F. R. ASIAT. SOC., F. R. AST. S.

AUTHOR OF CELTIC DRUIDS; APOLOGY FOR MOHAMED, THE ILLUSTRIOUS; ANACALYPSIS,
OR AN ENQUIRY INTO THE ORIGIN OF LANGUAGES, NATIONS AND RELIGIONS.

NEW YORK:
PETER ECKLER, PUBLISHER,
35 FULTON STREET.

PUBLISHER'S PREFACE.

IN *Horæ Sabbaticæ* the Christian Sabbath, or the Sunday, is shown, in the words of our learned author, "to be a *human*, not a *divine* institution,—a festival, not a day of humiliation,—to be kept by all consistent Christians with joy and gladness, like Christmas Day and Easter Sunday, and not like Ash Wednesday or Good Friday."

Strictly speaking, all institutions now observed by human beings may claim a human origin, but many pious and sincere people believe differently, and claim in addition to human laws, divine authority for the religious observance of Sunday. But their notions in regard to this subject are confused and ill-defined, and will not bear the test of examination.

They believe the Bible to be the inspired word of God, that Jesus Christ was the only-begotten Son of God, and also God himself, but when the Son of Mary defends his disciples for violating Jewish Sabbath laws by plucking corn on the Sabbath day, (as recorded in Mark ii, 23-28,) and tells the Pharisees that "The Sabbath was made for man and not man for the Sabbath," and that "the Son of man is Lord also of the Sabbath," our modern Sabbatarians, although they assert that "Jesus spoke as one having authority," yet seem to have no

sympathy with his liberal views, and, by striving to
enforce the puritanical Sunday laws of modern bigotry,
they, in effect, like the ancient Pharisees, oppose the
teachings of their "Saviour," and repudiate the authority of the God they pretend to worship.

Because the Jews were commanded in the Bible to "Remember [Saturday] the Sabbath day, to keep it holy,"
certain pharisaical sectarians decided to remember the *Sun*
day, the venerable day of the Sun, and keep it holy in
like manner, without any biblical command for so doing.

The Bible student will seek in vain throughout its
pages for any reference to Sunday observance, as there is
no authority whatever in either the Old or New Testament for keeping holy the day which the idolatrous
Pagans formerly dedicated to the Sun.   Christ and his
Disciples never proposed so radical an innovation.   St.
Paul and the Evangelists never advocated such a change.
The Apostles were Jews by birth, education, and faith.
They were strict observers of Jewish laws and customs,
and it was while celebrating the Jewish feast of the Passover at Jerusalem, that Jesus was betrayed by Judas,
and arrested, tried, convicted, and crucified by Pilate.

It is recorded of a certain pious Puritan of "Merrie
Old England," that he

" Hung a cat on Monday, for killing of a mouse on Sunday ; "

and it is certain that the Puritans of New England have,
by their pious zeal and odious Blue Laws, done all
within their power to make life a burden to the sojourner
within their gates on the day which the ancient Pagans

called *Sunday*, and which was observed by the Atheni-
ans as sacred to APOLLO, the Sun-god,—"the god of
life, and poesy, and light."

The first Christian Emperor, the wicked Constantine,
who imagined that his stalwart form, impressive features,
august and commanding presence, gave him a resemblance
to the Grecian HELIOS or Roman APOLLO,—the fabled
god of the Sun,—was a strong advocate for the change
from the Jewish sacred *Saturday* to the equally sacred
Pagan *Sunday*, or the day named for and dedicated to
the solar luminary. And when this latter day is observed
as a day of rest, recreation, or devotion, according to the
separate inclination of each and every individual, no
reasonable objection can be made to the change.

Sunday observance is at best but a human institution,
without any claim to occult authority, and while it is not
of special importance to wealthy people, who have the
365 days of the year at their disposal, it is of great ben-
efit and advantage to the industrial classes.

The religious orders, and all the followers of ancient
traditions, should be allowed the privilege of displaying
their faith in Sunday worship as ostentatiously as they
may desire, and reasonable people should not be molested
for observing Sunday in the manner which proves most
conducive to their welfare and happiness.

"One man," says St. Paul, "esteemeth one day above
another : another esteemeth every day *alike*. Let every
man be fully persuaded in his own mind."—*Rom. xiv, 5.*

PETER ECKLER.

PREFACE.

IN the following Treatise some persons perhaps may think, that too much trouble is taken to refute trifling objections: but the Author's object has been if possible to prevent reply. And he has not attempted to refute any objection, which has not at one time or other, been advanced by persons with whom he has argued on the subject.

He flatters himself that not one word will be found in the whole, which can give just offence to the orthodox or reasoning Christian, or even to the *sincere* follower of Wesley; though no doubt offence enough will be given to members of societies which suppress vice in rags, and cherish it in purple and fine raiment,—*itinerant* attendants at missionary meetings—such as practice *standing in the synagogues, and in the corners of the streets sounding their trumpet, and making long prayers.* (Matt. vi. 2-5. xxiii. 14, 15.) Persons well described in the following epigram, written by a much esteemed friend of the Author.

> How well the character agrees
> 'Twixt new and ancient pharisees;
> A surly, proud, vindictive race,
> Who spat upon our Saviour's face;
> Because he told them it was wrong
> Either to pray too loud, or long.

20 Keppel Street, Russell Square.

HORÆ SABBATICÆ.

—

O F the various rites which have been established by the founders of the different religions of the world, perhaps there is no one which is so intimately connected with the temporal happiness and comfort of mankind, as that of the observance of one day in every seven as a day of rest. The appropriation of certain days, at short periods of time, to the purposes of devotion, of recreation, and of relaxation from worldly cares, seems to be an institution peculiarly adapted to the improvement of the mind, and to the advancement of civilization. And yet the example of the Turks,—the strictest of all the observers of a Sabbath in modern times,—proves that, excellent as the institution is, human perverseness may prevail, to render it useless, to defeat the ends for which it probably was originally intended, and to destroy the good effects which it was so well calculated to produce.

2. The state of ignorance and barbarism, into which the inhabitants of the countries have fallen, which were formerly possessed by the elegant and enlightened caliphs, makes it evident that this institution is not necessarily accompanied with improvement and civilization;

and after its first institution amongst Christians, it was equally unavailable, to prevent the well-known ignorance and barbarism of the middle ages ; but in each case this effect has arisen by the abuse of it, or in opposition to it, not by its means. Its tendency was evidently to produce a contrary effect ; and it can only be regretted that its power was not greater and more efficacious.

3. But it is not fair to reason against the use, from the abuse of a thing ; and there is nothing in this world which may not be converted to an evil purpose, and the good effects of which may not be destroyed by artful and designing men. A proof of this may be found in the way in which attempts are now making in this country, to convert the institution of which I am treating to purposes pernicious in the highest degree to society — to make use of it to create or encourage a morose and gloomy superstition, the effect of which will be to debase, not to exalt or improve the human mind.

4. The Puritans, Evangelical Christians as they call themselves, the modern Pharisees in reality, a sect answering exactly to the Pharisees of old, finding that the restoration of the Jewish Sabbath, which was peculiarly ordained in the Old Testament for the use of the Jews, is well calculated to serve their purpose, and being precluded by various circumstances of their situation from having recourse to the expedients of the Catholic priests, to gain possession of the minds of their votaries, have exerted all their power by its means to attain this object. These are the reasons why we hear more of the heinous crime of Sabbath-breaking, than of all other vices to-

gether. And hence every nerve has been strained to the utmost, to extract from passages both in the Old and New Testament, meanings favorable to this design, which the words will not justify.* But the fair unsophisticated doctrines on this subject, as taught in these works, are what it is intended here to enquire into and discuss.

5. In the whole of the New Testament, a single passage cannot be discovered clearly directing the observance of a Sabbath. If this institution be of the importance which some persons attach to it in a religious point of view, it seems very extraordinary that not one of the Evangelists should have stated any thing clearly upon the subject:—very strange that we do not find the mode described in which it was kept by the first disciples, or the apostles, in plain, clear, and unequivocal language.

6. It seems reasonable to expect, that if the earliest Christians, the apostles or disciples, had considered that the observance of the Sunday was actually an exchange of the Sabbath from the Saturday, by divine appointment, we should find in the Acts of the Apostles all our doubts removed; and removed, not by implication or forced construction, but by a clear and unequivocal statement.

7. By the early Christians at first the Jewish Sabbath was strictly kept, but after some time it seems to have been considered by their immediate followers, along with

---

* No doubt, amongst the Pharisees of old, as amongst our Evangelical Christians, there were many good, well disposed persons, the dupes of the knaves.

all other Jewish ceremonies, to have been abolished ; but they appear very wisely to have thought, that it would be useful and proper to select one day in the week, which, without neglecting the ordinary duties of life arising out of their respective situations, should be appropriated to the observance of religious duties, of rest and recreation. This does not seem to have been the act of any regular deliberative meeting, but to have taken place by degrees, and to have been considered merely as a measure of discipline, liable at any time to be varied or omitted, as the heads of the religion might think was expedient.

8. From a variety of passages in the Gospels, Jesus appears in his actions to have made no distinction betwixt the Sabbath and any other day; doing the same things on the Sabbath that he did on any other day. In reply to this it is said, that what he did on the Sabbath was good and useful—such as healing the sick : this is true ; but he did nothing on any other day which was not good and useful ; and therefore nothing in favor of the Sabbath can be inferred from this. Every thing which is not bad is good ; and it is wrong to do any thing on any day which is not good. One of the most important of all the Jewish rites, and one of the most strictly enforced by the Pharisees, was the observance of the Sabbath ; and it appears evident, that Jesus performed various actions for the express purpose of making manifest his disapprobation of the strict observance of this rite, or indeed of its observance at all.

9. After he had healed the sick man at the pool of Bethesda, he ordered him to remove his bed on the Sabbath-day; and it appears from John v. 10, 11, 12, that a very correct and marked distinction was made by the Jews, betwixt healing the man and carrying away the bed : they say,

It is the Sabbath ; it is not lawful for thee to take up thy couch.

Afterward, when the Jews charged Jesus with having broken the Sabbath in this instance, his reply was very extraordinary : v. 17.

My Father worketh until now, and I work.

10. If the doctrine of Jesus be deduced by implication from his conduct, from this very instance the Sabbath must be held to be abolished. He expressly says to the observation on the subject of the couch, "*I work.*" The answer of Jesus clearly applies to the moving the bed as well as healing the man ; because the expression is, "these things," in the plural number; and there were but two acts which could be referred to.

11. But another observation offers itself on this subject : here is the fairest opportunity afforded to Jesus to support the Sabbath, if he had thought proper. If he had thought it right that the Sabbath should have been continued, he would have said to the sick man, Arise, and walk, and remove thy bed when the Sabbath is over. He would then have taught in the clearest and shortest

terms possible, the propriety of doing good works of
necessity, and the impropriety of doing such as were not
works of necessity on the Sabbath. In every one of the
following texts, an opportunity is afforded to Jesus, so
favorable for the inculcation of the observance of the
Sabbath, that it is very difficult to account for his neglect of it, if it were his intention that it should be continued.

Luke xiv, 4, 5. xiii. 14. vi. 6-10. Matt. xii. 2. Mark, ii. 27.
John vii. 22. ix. 16.

12. Jesus constantly evades the attacks of the Jews on
the ground of necessity ; but in no instance does he drop
a word expressive of disapprobation, of *doing even unnecessary* works on the Sabbath. This is named, though
it is not necessary to the argument ; because if he had
expressed himself against doing unnecessary works on
the Jewish Sabbath, no consequence could be drawn
from this circumstance respecting the Christian observance of Sunday.

13. In Luke xviii. Jesus has an opportunity of a
different kind from the above, of supporting the Sabbath : but he avoids it.

18. A certain ruler asked him, saying, Good Master, what
shall I do to inherit eternal life?

19. And Jesus said unto him, Why callest thou me good?
none is good, save one, that is God.

20. Thou knowest the commandments, Do not commit
adultery, Do not kill, Do not steal, Do not bear false witness,
Honor thy father and thy mother.

21. And he said, All these have I kept from my youth up.

22. Now, when Jesus heard these things, he said unto him, Yet lackest thou one thing ; sell all that thou hast, and give to the poor, &c.

14. Here Jesus not only avoids directing the observance of the Sabbath ; but in actually specifying the commandments by name which are necessary to insure salvation, and omitting the Sabbath, if he do not actually abolish it the neglect of the opportunity of inculcating it, raises by implication a strong presumption against it. But, indeed, in not adding the observance of the Sabbath to the one thing more which was lacking, he actually abolishes it, if the common signification of words is to be received.

15. The ordering the bed to be removed was one breach of the Sabbath, and the following passage exhibits a second example of a premeditated breach of it by Jesus.

16. At the first verse of the sixth chapter of Luke it is written,

And it came to pass, on the first Sabbath after the second day of unleavened bread, that he went through the corn-fields ; and his disciples plucked the ears of corn, and did eat, rubbing them with their hands.

17. In this passage it appears, that the disciples of Jesus, with his approbation, reaped the corn on a Sabbath-day. It also appears that he was travelling on that day. The Pharisees, as usual, reprimanded him for breaking the Sabbath, which he justified, saying, "The Son of man is Lord even of the Sabbath," ver. 5.

18. It cannot be supposed that provisions were not to be had in Judea. It is represented to have been almost incredibly rich and populous: and if Jesus had not thought the reaping the corn on the Sabbath justifiable, he would have provided against the necessity of doing it, if any necessity there was. He might also have made use of this occasion to inculcate the doctrine, that though acts of necessity were permitted, all others were expressly forbidden on the Sabbath-day. It is very evident that he was travelling. The road probably as at this day passed through the open corn-fields.

And it came to pass that he went through the corn-fields on the Sabbath ; and his disciples began as they went to pluck the ears of corn; and the Pharisees said unto him, See, why do they on the Sabbath that which is not lawful?*

19. The conduct of his disciples he defends, upon the example of David eating the shew-bread, which it was lawful only for the priests to eat; and adds, that the Sabbath was made for man, not man for the Sabbath. But not a word is said which can be construed in favor of *keeping* the Sabbath.

20. It has been observed that only the burthensome parts of the Jewish law were abolished, but that the observance of the Sabbath is not a burthen. Where is the authority for this? Is it not a burthen to be refused permission to cut the wheat when it is shaking, or to

---

* By this it was not meant that they were doing an unlawful act because the corn was not their own, but by Sabbath-breaking. To pluck the ears of corn is permitted by Deut. xxiii., 25.

carry it from the approaching storm? all which is expressly forbidden on the Jewish Sabbath.

21. The abolition of the Levitical law was intended, but Jesus no where expressly declared it to be so. The same reason operated in the case of the abolition of the Levitical law as in the abolition of the Sabbath, to prevent him publicly declaring it.

22. If Jesus had expressly declared that people were to work on the Sabbath, and that it was to be abolished, he would have offended against the 31st chapter and 15th verse of Exodus.

Whosoever doeth any work in the Sabbath-day, he shall surely be put to death.

23. Indeed the strongest charges brought by the Jews against him were, that he had broken the Sabbath, and attempted the overthrow of the Levitical law. John says, v. 18.

Wherefore the Jews sought the more to kill him, because he not only had *broken* the Sabbath, but said also, that God was his father.

24. If any Jew attempted to destroy the law and constitution as established by Moses, he was clearly by that law liable to suffer the punishment of death. Exod. xxxi. 15. Numbers xv. 32. Deut. xiii. xxx. xxxi. 14–18.

25. And that such was the intention of the mission of Jesus is clearly proved by the result, with which we are all acquainted, as well as by the decision of the Apostles

detailed in the book of their Acts, by which the whole
of the old law is abolished, except four things, which
are called necessary.

26. The Apostles must have known from Jesus what
was his intention; besides, acting under the direction
of the Holy Spirit, they could not err. When Jesus
abolished the old law, of course he abolished every part
of it which was not expressly excepted.

In Matt. v. 17. Jesus says, *Think not that I am come to
destroy the law,* &c., but to fulfill it.

27. This expression appears peculiarly clear and appropriate: and it seems extraordinary, that the learned
and ingenious Unitarian, Mr. Evanson, should have
found any difficulty in it.

28. According to the account given of Jesus in the
Gospels, it was evidently not his inclination to surrender
himself to the Jews, until a particular period, when his
mission had become fulfilled; for this reason it was,
that he repeatedly withdrew from them privately, when
their rage threatened his life: for the same reason, he
constantly spoke equivocally when he saw there was
danger in speaking clearly, until the last moment, when
he openly avowed himself to Pilate to be the Messiah.
The question whether he came to abolish the old law
was evidently a snare; and if he had answered it in the
affirmative, he would have been instantly liable to suffer
death, according to the law given by God in Leviticus,
and which he came to abolish: but the answer he gave
was ambiguous to the Jews at that time, although clear

to us now, if the correct meaning of the words be attended to.

29. God entered into a covenant with the Jews to continue until the coming of the Messiah.*

30. Suppose I enter into a covenant with a man, to take a farm of me on certain terms for seven years. At the end of this time, is the covenant abolished? No. Are the terms or laws on which he held the farm abolished? No. The law or terms, as well as the covenant, are fulfilled, not abolished; and, as the lawyers would say, the demise is determined. The word fufilled is the proper and true word to use, and if the word abolished or destroyed had been substituted, it would have been wrong and untrue; and as the institution of the Sabbath was a part of the revealed law, or commandment of God, and was in no other way obligatory than the remainder of the old law, of course it falls under exactly the same rule, and as it was not excepted, was with it fulfilled.

31. It has been said that the instances produced of Sabbath-breaking by Jesus and his disciples, are of so trifling a nature, that nothing can be implied from them. On the contrary, they were evidently done for the sake of *agitating* the question of the Sabbath; and if something important did not depend upon them, they are much too trifling to have been noticed at all. In each of the cases they are named, evidently for the sake of affording an opportunity, to record the expression of Jesus to the Pharisees, which came from him in the

*See Matt. v. 17.

conversation which followed his act. The removal of the bed was no part of the miracle, and was totally and absolutely unnecessary, and directly in defiance of the old law. The act of pulling the corn, allowed by Deut. xxiii. 25, was equally an unnecessary act; for if it belonged to his disciples, their residence must have been within a few minutes' walk; and if it did not, it must have been in the centre of a populous country; and if it were further than about one mile (a Sabbath-day's journey) from the place where Jesus rested the preceding night, he must have been guilty of a breach of the Sabbath, of a most remarkable and unequivocal description, in travelling further than allowed by the law on the Sabbath-day.

32. In order to form a judgment of the great consequence, which ought to be attached to the act of breaking the Sabbath by Jesus, it will be useful to consider, in what light it was viewed by the old law, and by the Jews with God's approbation: the reader will then see, that the act of Jesus must in him be considered of the first consequence; not as a trifle, as we at this day consider reaping corn or moving a bed. The following verses will set this in its proper light. Numbers xv.

32. And while the children of Israel were in the wilderness, they found a man that gathered sticks upon the Sabbath-day.

33. And they that found him gathering sticks brought him unto Moses and Aaron, and unto all the congregation:

34. And they put him in ward, because it was not declared what should be done unto him.

35. And the Lord said unto Moses, The man shall be surely

put to death : all the congregation shall stone him with stones without the camp.

36. And all the congregation brought him without the camp, and stoned him with stones, and he died; as the Lord commanded Moses.

33. If the character of Jesus be considered, it is very absurd to contend, that any act of his, recorded by the pen of an inspired writer, ought to be lightly estimated : this is actual profaneness in a Christian. It is incumbent on every believer in his divine mission to look upon each action of his life as an action recorded for the purpose of example, or of affording an opportunity of inculcating some doctrine : and as such, the moving of a bed, or travelling, or pulling corn on the Sabbath, become circumstances of great moment, when recorded by the pen of an inspired writer.

34. It has been said, that Jesus by preaching in the synagogue on that day kept the Sabbath. If this argument be good for any thing, it shows that the Saturday, not the Sunday, ought to be kept. But in fact this proves nothing with respect either to the Saturday or Sunday ; for in preaching on the Sabbath-day, he only did what he did on every other day of the week ; and he evidently went into the synagogue because there the Jews were collected together. He was circumcised, and kept *all* the Jewish feasts and rites of the old law (unless the Sabbath be excepted); then if the Sabbath ought to be kept by Christians because he kept it, all the rites and ceremonies of the old law ought to be followed, because he followed them. This is the necessary consequence if

persons reason consistently from cause to effect.   As Dr.
Paley correctly observes,

'If the command by which the Sabbath was instituted be
binding upon Christians, it must bind as to the day, the duties,
and the penalty ; in none of which is it received.'

35. The fact is, that his conduct appeared to be so
equivocal to many of the Jewish Christians at that time,
that they continued to observe the Jewish law with all
its burthensome rites and ceremonies, until the council
of the Apostles at Jerusalem, acting under the direction
of the Holy Ghost, and speaking by the mouth of St.
Paul to the citizens of Antioch, abolished the whole
except four things.

36. It appears from chapter the 15th of the Acts, that
it was proposed that the Gentile converts should observe
the law of Moses.   Upon this a difference of opinion
arose.   Now there can be no doubt that if the Sabbath,
or any other part of the old law were to be retained, it
would have been here expressed : but the Apostles only
require from the Gentiles to observe four things, which
they call necessary, and expressly absolve them from the
remainder; and the observance of the Sabbath is not
one of the four excepted.

37. The Sabbath is a Jewish rite, not a moral law,
and every such rite is expressly abolished.   As the
Decalogue, which is a part of the Jewish law, is not
excepted, and depends on precisely the same authority as
all the remainder, it must be held, *unless it be specifically
excepted* as a CODE of law, to be abolished also : and the

moral laws which are intermixed with the Jewish rites which it contains, must be held to depend upon their own truth or the commands of Jesus.

28. For it hath seemed good to the Holy Spirit and to us, to lay upon you no greater burthen than these necessary things :   .

29. That ye abstain from things offered to idols, and from blood, *and from things strangled, and from fornication;* from which if you keep yourselves, ye will do well. Acts xv. 28, also xxi. 25.

38. It is here worthy of observation, that the part marked in Italics is no part of the Decalogue.

39. Again, in Acts xxi. 25, the question respecting the observance of the old law is alluded to, and it is expressly forbidden.

25. As touching the Gentiles which believe, we have written and concluded, that they observe no such thing, save only that they keep themselves from things offered to idols, and from blood, and from strangled, and from fornication.

40. Here, as it is a part of the old law, it is actually expressly forbidden. The Apostles, acting under the influence of the Holy Spirit, and speaking of the old law —the whole of it—say, *We have concluded that they observe no such thing.*

41. How can words of prohibition be more clear than these? NO SUCH THING ; save only, &c. If by explanation the Sabbath can be shown to be continued, there is no expression in any language which may not be explained to mean directly the reverse of what the speaker intended.

42. This is quite enough to decide the question ; but we will see what St. Paul thought of it.

43. Of course all Christians of the present day will allow, that where a doubt shall exist respecting the meaning of the Gospels, or of Jesus himself, if St. Paul have expounded it or explained it, his authority must be conclusive and binding upon them. In the following two verses, St. Paul has actually declared that the Sabbath was abolished:

8. Owe no man any thing, but to love one another : for he that loveth another hath fulfilled the law.

9. For this, Thou shalt not commit adultery, Thou shalt not kill, Thou shalt not steal, Thou shalt not bear false witness, Thou shalt not covet; and if there be any other commandment, it is briefly comprehended in this saying, namely, Thou shalt love thy neighbour as thyself.—Rom. xiii, 8, 9.

44. If there be any other commandment, it is what? Not the observance of the, or a, Sabbath. How can any thing be clearer than this? Besides, it is evident that in his letter of instruction to the Romans, he would have told them that they were to keep a day in lieu of it, if he had thought it imperative on them so to do. If St. Paul be authority, every commandment in Genesis or elsewhere in the Old Testament is expressly abolished.

45. But in the following passage St. Paul goes much further, and not only abolishes the Sabbath, but actually declares himself against the compulsory use of days altogether as *necessary* appendages or parts of religion. St. Paul could not fail to know that the observance of days might be converted to the purposes of superstition,

the same as all other forms and ceremonies had been by some of the Pharisees, and other hypocritical pretenders to superior sanctity, to the exclusion or neglect of true devotion and the moral law.

5. One man esteemeth one day above another; another esteemeth every day alike. Let every man be fully persuaded in his own mind.
6. He that regardeth the day, regardeth it unto the Lord. And he that regardeth not the day, to the Lord he doth not regard it.— Rom. xiv. 5, 6.

46. Here, unless we distort the meaning of plain words, St. Paul abolishes the compulsory observance of days, or states the observance of them not to be necessary ; but as the observance of certain days may evidently have no guilt in it, he says, If you think it right to keep them, it is well ; but if you think otherwise, it is also well. In both cases, *it is to the Lord*, to use his mode of expression.

47. In the second chapter of the Epistle to the Colossians, verse 16, is a passage in which St. Paul again expresses himself against the observance of fixed days, or Sabbaths.

48. Dr. Paley prefaces his quotation of this text with the following observation : and no person but as degraded a fanatic as Johanna Southcote, or the modern ranters, will treat the opinion of the venerable Paley with disrespect. He says,

'St. Paul evidently appears to have considered the Sabbath as part of the Jewish ritual, and not obligatory upon Christians.'

49. If St. Paul have *evidently* decided the question, surely Christians may safely rest upon his authority: he says,

16. Let no man therefore judge you in meat, or in drink, or in respect of an holiday, or of the new moon, or of the Sabbath days ;
17. Which are a shadow of things to come : but the body is of Christ.

50. By the use of meats or drinks, he must allude to the use of them on fast-days, because the use of them on other days no man ever said was wrong. The same argument must apply to the neglect of feast-days regulated by the state of the moon. The same of the Sabbath ; for it is not maintained that there was any guilt in keeping a day of rest: the offence was in breaking it : and here St. Paul must be construed to mean, Let no man condemn you for the breach of the Sabbath. It seems absurd to construe it to mean, Let no man condemn you because you choose to keep a Sabbath or day of rest. If it be so construed, then it must also be said, (to be consistent,) Let no man condemn you for merely taking necessary food. If it do not mean, Let no man condemn you for taking meat on some days when it is forbidden, it is actual nonsense. But in a few verses he seems to explain his own meaning.

20. If ye be dead with Christ from the rudiments of the world, why, as though living in the world, are ye subject to ordinances,
21. (Touch not, taste not, handle not:
22. Which all are to perish with the using,) after the commandments and doctrines of men?

23. Which things have indeed a show of wisdom in will-worship and humility, and neglecting of the body ; not in any honour to the satisfying of the flesh.

51. In the next chapter he goes on to direct the Colossians to seek those things which are above.

Mind the things above, not the things below, &c.

52. The whole of this train of reasoning is consistent with itself, and also with what he has said in the Epistle to the Romans, xiv.

He who regardeth the day, regardeth it to the Lord; and he who regardeth not the day, to the Lord he regardeth it not.

53. The whole of St. Paul's preaching goes to inculcate that the observance of feasts and fasts is a matter merely optional, and that the observance or non-observance of them is no offence, and consequently he is directly against the compelling their observance by law.

54 In the whole of the Epistles, there does not seem to be a single clear, unequivocal passage in favor of the Sabbath. In almost numberless places breakers of such of the commandments as are in themselves moral rules, independent of the law of Moses, are condemned in the strongest terms : for example, 1 Cor. vi. 9, 10. Gal. v. 19—21. 2 Tim. iii. 2.

55. But in not one of them is a Sabbath-breaker named. How does this happen? The reason is sufficiently plain. The breach of the Sabbath under the old law was a breach of the covenant with God, and therefore a high offence; but the Sabbath being abolished, under the new law it was none.

56. Although Dr. Paley does not agree with the author entirely respecting the Lord's-day, he makes several admissions, which, coming from him, are very important. He says,

'A cessation upon that day (meaning Sunday) from labor, beyond the time of attendance upon public worship, is not intimated in any passage of the New Testament; nor did Christ or his Apostles deliver, that we know of, any command to their disciples for a discontinuance upon that day of the common offices of their professions.'

57. Upon this it may be observed, neither is the necessity of attendance upon public worship intimated particularly upon that day, in preference to any *other*. Nothing is said upon the subject, therefore nothing can be inferred. So that the proof of the necessity of attendance on divine worship must be sought for elsewhere.* In fact, the non-inculcation of public worship

---

*In the four Gospels, no person can point out a single passage which, in clear unequivocal terms, directs the observance of *public* worship. One text may be shown where it is tolerated;

Where two or three are gathered together in one place, I will grant their request.

And one where it is discouraged, at the least, if it be not expressly prohibited; and where such persons as may not think it necessary, are expressly justified for its non-observance:

5. And when thou prayest, thou shalt not be as the hypocrites are: for they love to pray standing in the synagogues, and in the corners of the streets, that they may be seen of men. Verily I say unto you, they have their reward.
6. But thou, when thou prayest, enter into thy closet; and when thou hast shut thy door, pray to thy Father which is in secret; and thy Father, which seeth in secret, shall reward thee openly.— Matt. vi. 5, 6.

Except these two texts in the Gospel, the author knows not one which alludes to public worship: — a thing with pageantry, &c., &c., as much abused sometimes by Christians, as ever it was by Jews or Heathens. The attendance of Jesus in the synagogues can no more be cited to support it, than his observance of the passover and other Jewish rites can be cited to support the rest of the laws of Leviticus abolished by the Acts.

in the passages alluded to above, proves nothing either for or against it: only it goes to prove that it was not particularly ordered on the first day, more than on the seventh or any other day, and leaves the times for its observance open to be fixed on what days the government, or the rulers of the churches think proper.—What is said here must not be construed as a wish to prohibit all public worship; but only to place it on a correct footing as a right of discipline, and to discourage the fashionable pharisaical doctrine, that all merit is included in praying in *the synagogues, and at the corners of the streets*, and making long speeches at Bible Society meetings, &c.

Again, Paley says, ' The opinion, that Christ and his Apostles meant to retain the duties of the Jewish Sabbath, shifting only the day from the seventh to the first, seems to prevail without sufficient proof; nor does any evidence remain in Scripture, (of what, however, is not improbable) that the first day of the week was thus distinguished in commemoration of our Lord's resurrection.'— Mor. Phil. p. 337. Ed. 8vo.

58. Certainly *in Scripture* there is no evidence.

59. In this view of the doctrines of St. Paul the author is happy to have so learned and respectable a divine as Michaelis of his opinion. And indeed as the opinion of Michaelis is not objected to by Bishop Marsh, his translator, in his usual way by a note, where he disapproves any thing, the author seems to have a right to claim him also.

Michaelis, chap. xv. s. 3. says, ' The Epistle to the Colossians resembles that to the Ephesians, both in its contents and in its language, so that the one illustrates the other. In all three, the Apostle shows the superiority of Christ to the Angels, and warns the Christians against the worship of Angels. *He censures the observation of Sabbaths*, rebukes those who forbid marriage, and the touching of certain things, who deliver commandments of men concerning meats, and prohibit them.*

60. Some well-meaning persons, looking about for any thing which might aid them in the support of the early prejudices of their nurseries and education, have fancied, that they could find a Sabbath in the practice of the Apostles of meeting together on the first day of the week. This question we will now examine, and see whether they, on that day, did meet, and if from these meetings a rite of such prodigious importance as the renovation of the Jewish Sabbath can be inferred.

61. There are only three passages in the New Testament, which make mention of the Apostles' being assembled on the first day of the week. The first is on the day of the resurrection, John xx. 19.

19. Then the same day at evening, being the first day of the week, when the doors were shut where the disciples were

---

* It gives the author great satisfaction to have an opportunity of bearing his humble testimony to the conduct of Michaelis and Bishop Marsh. In reading their works, his pleasure is never diminished by the fear of wilful misrepresentation, economical reasoning, or false quotation. They are as superior to most of their predecessors or cotemporaries in integrity, as they are in talent. His Lordship has been seldom out of polemical warfare, and has experienced the usual vicissitudes of victory and defeat (the later for instance by Gandolphy); but conqueror or conquered, he has never stooped to the meanness of a pious fraud. It is one of the misfortunes of the author, never to have had the opportunity either to speak to or to see the venerable Bishop, one of the greatest ornaments of the bench in the present day.

assembled for fear of the Jews, came Jesus, and stood in the midst of them.

62. Jesus Christ is described to have risen that day before day-light in the morning, and after all the various events which in the course of the first part of that eventful day had happened to several of them, it was very natural that they should assemble together as soon as possible, to confer respecting them, and to consider what was the proper line of conduct for them to pursue. It is absurd to suppose that this assembly could be held to celebrate the rites of the religion, before the Apostles were all of them satisfied that he had risen, and that his body had not been stolen, as it is stated that some of them at first suspected. The peculiar accidental circumstances evidently caused this meeting to be held as soon as possible after the resurrection, and it would have been the fourth or any other day, if Jesus had happened to have arisen on that day.

63. But it is necessary to observe, for the information of such persons as have not made the Jewish customs and antiquities their study, that the computation of time amongst the Jews was very different from ours; and it is evidently necessary to consider the words of the texts with reference to their customs, not to ours. Our day begins at or after twelve o'clock at night, theirs began at or after six o'clock in the evening. In Genesis it is said, And the evening and the morning were the first day. If the day had begun as ours does, it would have said, The morning and the evening were the first day; and in Levit. xxiii. 32, it is said, *From even to even shall*

you celebrate your Sabbath; consequently, the Jewish
Sabbath began on Friday evening at about six o'clock,
and their supper, or, as it is called, their breaking of
bread, took place immediately after; the candles being
ready lighted, and the viands being placed on the tables,
so that no work by the servants might be necessary;
and there they remained on the tables till after six the
next evening. The custom of breaking bread in token
of amity and brotherly love, was an old custom of the
Jews, something like the giving of salt amongst the
Arabians, and is continued amongst them to this day.

64. By the word day two clear and distinct ideas are
expressed; it means the light part of the twenty-four
hours, in opposition to the dark part of them, and it
means the period itself of the twenty-four hours—one
revolution of the earth upon its axis.

65. In the expression here, *the same day at evening,*
the word day must mean, the day-light part of the day,
in opposition to the dark part of it—the night; because
Jesus *could* not have appeared literally on the evening of
the first day of the week; that is, after six o'clock on
the Saturday evening, he not having risen at that time;
therefore this meeting, being probably after six o'clock
in the evening, on account of the return of the two
Apostles from Emmaus that day, the day of the resurrection, Luke xxiv. 30; it, in fact, must have taken place,
though on the first day-light day, a little before sunset;
yet, on the second, not on the first Jewish day of the
week. It is not surprising that persons should find a
difficulty in clearing their minds from the prejudices,

created by long habit and education, respecting the question and expression of the first day of the week. But if they will only give themselves the trouble *carefully* to examine, the truth must prevail.

66. For these various reasons, whether the meeting named in John xx. 19, be considered the first day of the week, or the second, no inference in favor of a Sabbatical observance of the Sunday can be deduced: for it was merely accidental whether it were the first day or the second.

67. In the 26th verse of the twentieth chapter of John, it is said,

And after eight days again his disciples were within, and Thomas with them.

68. Whether the meeting above alluded to was on the first or second day of the week, it does not seem clear how this, the day after eight days, should be the first, *i. e.* the eighth day. It may have been the ninth in one case, and the tenth in the other; but in no case can it have been the first or the eighth day. If this passage meant to describe the meeting to have been on the first day of the week, it would have said, On the first day; or, After several days; or, On the day after the Sabbath. The expression evidently proves that it could not be the first.

69. The next passage, which is in the Acts of the Apostles, xx. 7, is as follows:

And upon the first day of the week, when the disciples came together to break bread, Paul preached unto them (ready to depart on the morrow), and continued his speech until mid-night.

70. As a learned layman, in his controversy with Dr. Priestley, has justly observed : This meeting, according to the Jewish custom, and form of language, and computation of time, could have taken place at no other time than after six o'clock on Saturday evening : there was but one time, viz. the evening of each day, when they met for the purpose of breaking of bread ; and it therefore necessarily follows, that the preaching of Paul must have taken place on the Saturday night, after six o'clock, by our mode of computation, ready to depart on the morrow, at day-break. Surely the preaching of Paul on Saturday night, and his travelling on the Sunday, cannot be construed into a proof that he kept the Sunday as a Sabbath.

71. In the only subsequent passage where the first day of the week is named, 1 Cor. xvi. 2, the same gentleman has shown, that if any inference is to be drawn from the words contained in it, they go against the observance of it as a Sabbath, and imply that a man on that day was to settle his accounts of the week preceding, that he might be able to ascertain what he could lay up in store against Paul came.

Upon the first day of the week let every one of you lay by him in store, as God hath prospered him, that there be no gatherings when I come.

72. How can any one see in this verse, a proof that the first day of the week was to be kept by Christians as an obligation, as a Jewish Sabbath ? It is well known that

at first the Christians strictly kept the Jewish Sabbath; therefore they could not make a weekly settlement of their accounts till the day after the Sabbath, which was the first. It is observed by the same learned person, in his controversy with Dr. Priestley,

'I would as soon misspend my time in attempting to prove that the sun shone at noon-day, to a person who should persist in affirming it to be then midnight-darkness, as I would contend with any one who will assert, that an express precept for a man to lay by money, *in his own custody*, signifies that he should deposit it, *in the custody of another person:* or who, well knowing that in the time of the Apostles, the hour of assembling together, both for their ordinary chief meal, and for the celebration of the Lord's supper, was in the evening, at the beginning of the Jewish day, persists in maintaining, that a predication which St. Luke informs us took place at that particular time, did not commence then, but at an hour when they never assembled for those purposes. I will, therefore, only remark, on the latter instance, that I am sorry to appear so ignorant to Dr. Priestley, as not to have known, that amongst the Jews, as in every other nation, the word day was used sometimes to denote the periodical revolution of twenty-four hours; at others to express *day-light*, in opposition to darkness or night. I am sure the force of my argument required that it should be so understood. And I only quoted the beginning of Acts iv. to convince Subsidiarius, whose head seemed to be prepossessed with modern English ideas, that though the word morrow, or morning, in our language signifies the next civil day, because our evening and subsequent morning are in different days, yet, amongst the Jews, when opposed to the preceding night or evening, it meant the same civil day; because, with them, the evening and following morning were in the same day.'

73. The texts here cited being disposed of, it is only necessary to observe, that there is not the smallest evidence to be found, either positive or presumptive,

that the *Apostles or disciples* of Jesus considered the first day of the week in any way whatever different from the following five.

74. In the two first Epistles of John will be found many passages inculcating obedience to the commandments of God, and of Jesus in general terms, and specifying some ordinances as commandments, which are not to be found in the Decalogue, v. 15 : whence it appears that the word commandment cannot be construed to apply exclusively to the Decalogue, or to mean any one commandment in particular; especially one like the observance of the Sabbath, that is not binding by any moral law,—one which must depend entirely, either in the old or new law, upon a specific revelation, and not upon the general principles of morality which have been acknowledged in all ages and nations,—one which is actually, as has been shown in the Acts, xv. 28, specifically abolished by Jesus,—and one which, by the the instances of the miracle of the pool of Bethesda and the reaping of the corn, is also abolished, if any rule of conduct can be deduced from his actions.

75. If there be two ways of construing the New Testament, or any work whatever, one of which makes it totally inconsistent with itself, and the other consistent, common sense dictates, that the latter should be adopted. Now if we maintain that by commandments all the Decalogue or the orders in Leviticus are meant, we expressly contradict the passage of the Acts, where all the old law is abolished except four particulars, and we make the book inconsistent with itself. But if we

construe it, that in this passage of John the word commandment only means these which are excepted, and
those given in addition by Jesus, the whole is consistent.

76. It cannot be said that by this the laws of morality
laid down in the Decalogue are abolished, because if
they did not remain firm on the general principles of the
moral law of all nations, yet every law of morality
essential to the welfare of mankind, is excepted from
· the abolition in various places; for instance, in 1 Cor.
vi. 9, 10, Gal. v. 19, 20, 2 Tim. iii. 2, where particular
parts of the old law are alluded to and re-enacted, and in
1 John iii. 23, iv. 21, where new commandments of
morality are given much superior to some of the old
ones, and the meaning of the word commandment is
actually explained.

77. By this reasoning we are no longer encumbered
with some parts of the Decalogue, which, to say the
least of them, it is not easy to explain in a manner
satisfactory to the minds of young persons, and even of
many serious thinking persons of more mature age;
who find a difficulty in reconciling their minds to such
passages as that relating to a jealous God; a passage
merely applicable to the Jews.

78. Some persons have supposed, that the word commandments in the Old Testament necessarily means the
Decalogue, and the Decalogue exclusively. This interpretation cannot be supported, because the word commandment is used in its common or usual sense as a
command or order of God, before the Decalogue was
given, as in Exod. xvi. 28.

And the Lord said unto Moses, How long refuse ye to keep my commandments and my laws?

79. The pious Christian will not forget, that the moral law is not entirely dependent either on the law of Moses or of Christ; though they have confirmed it, yet it was binding on all mankind before Moses or Jesus were either of them born. Although there were no Jews or Christians, can it be supposed that the moral law, the law of right and wrong, was unknown to Abraham and the patriarchs before him? This would indeed be absurd enough. It must be also recollected, that the whole law of morality is not contained in the Decalogue; and yet the breach of this law, although in instances where it is not named in that code, is a sin, both to Jews and others.

80. Nor will a man be held blameless if he keep all the laws of the Decalogue, and commit some sins not therein named. For there are several HEINOUS SINS not named in that code. All the sins against the moral law prohibited in the Decalogue, and several others therein not named, are forbidden by Jesus and Paul over and over again. Therefore, as a code of law, what loss can the abolition of the Decalogue be? Is not the new law which God delivered by Jesus, as binding as that delivered by Moses?

81. It is well known that the version of the Pentateuch called the Septuagint, was anciently translated from the Hebrew into the Greek language, by certain Jews, either for the use of Ptolemy Philadelphus, or of their countrymen residing at Alexandria. When these persons came to the translation of the word Jehovah, they found

themselves in a difficulty; for it was an acknowledged doctrine of their religion, never disputed by any of their prophets or priests, that this name, by which God had thought proper to designate himself in the third verse of the sixth chapter of Exodus, ought never to be written or spoken upon any occasion, except the most awful and important. And it is the use or abuse of this particular name of God, to which the Jews always understood the command of the Decalogue to apply, which we render by the words, *Thou shalt not take the name of the Lord thy God in vain.* But which ought to be rendered, *Thou shalt not take the name of* JEHOVAH *thy God in vain.* This word, Jehovah, was inscribed on the golden plate on the forehead of the High-priest, when he entered the Holy of Holies, and also on his breast plate : and lest it should suffer any change, it was written in the Samaritan letters, those in which the Pentateuch was originally written, and from which it was translated into Hebrew by Ezra, after the Captivity. In the time of St. Jerom, it still continued written in many Hebrew and Greek Bibles in the Samaritan character. When the Jews came to this word in their translation, in order to avoid the profaneness of writing it literally, they adopted the word Κύριος, or Lord ; and thus got over the difficulty. But this contrivance does not in any way alter the nature of the command of the Decalogue, which still continues in all its original force applicable to the Jews, and to all Christians too, if they maintain the Decalogue to be excepted from the abolition of the other commandments of God in Exodus and Leviticus. Christians say this

interpretation of the word is only an idle superstition of
the Jews. It is no more idle superstition to them, than
is the prohibition to sow blended corn, or plough with
an ox yoked to an ass. It is an idle superstition to the
Christian, because Jesus abolished it in not excepting it.
If Jesus did not abolish the Decalogue as a code of law,
then we must no more write the word Jehovah : for the
Decalogue applies solely to the use of the word Jehovah,
and not to our disgraceful and odious habit of profane
swearing, to which our modern translators have applied
it. Does the considerate and unprejudiced Christian
really think, that Jesus intended this doctrine respecting
the use of the word Jehovah to be continued by Christians? What has been said respecting the word Jehovah
in the Decalogue cannot be disputed ; and when Christian priests call the construction given to it by the Jews
an idle superstition, they surely can neither be praised
for their piety nor for their prudence. The reverence
for the peculiar name *Jehovah* commanded to the Jews,
was one of those things not intended to be continued
under the Christian dispensation, and therefore was not
excepted by Jesus, when he was abolishing the Jewish
code. And the very circumstance shows that the Decalogue as a code of law was not intended to be continued.
In translating the Old Testament, Christians do wrong
in not translating the word Jehovah literally. The Jews
were not only excusable in translating it by the word
Lord, but they would have been sinful if they had translated it literally.

82. Persons must not entertain the idea, that because

the ten laws in the Decalogue were intended solely for the Jews, the laws of *morality* were not binding upon others. They were bound by them just as much as if the Decalogue had never been promulgated. If the Decalogue AS A CODE of law were binding upon the Gentiles, then were they bound to keep the Sabbath; and surely no one can pretend that that was ever intended, or that a single word in all the Bible can be shown expressive of disapprobation of the conduct of the Gentiles in not keeping it. Persons reasoning correctly, must remember that the observance of a Sabbath is not a *moral* law, but a rite of discipline.

83. The Decalogue was no more binding on the Jews, than any other of God's commands. There can be no distinction or preference of one command to another. *All the commands of God are alike entitled to instant unqualified obedience.* Nor can any doctrine so contrary to the character of God, be deduced from the giving of the Decalogue by him to the Jews, as that, of one command being more worthy of obedience than another.

84. The state of the case with the Decalogue is precisely like what often takes place with the English law. The Parliament, for reasons sometimes good and sometimes bad, passes a declaratory act to declare what the law is, or perhaps to increase the penalties for an offence. This act then becomes a part of the English code. It afterward passes an act to repeal this act; by this the law reverts to its original state, as if no such act had ever been passed. This was the case with respect to the doctrine of the Trinity; an act was passed to declare or

to increase the penalties for impugning it; that act has
been repealed; but the judges have declared, that though
that act has been repealed, it is still, at common law, an
offence to impugn the Trinity, and that it is punishable
by them. Thus, when the Decalogue as *a code of law*
was abrogated, the laws of morality reverted to exactly
what they were in the time of Abraham; and as such
they remain to Christians, unless Jesus added any thing
to them; and this we know that he did; for he expressly
says, A new commandment give I unto you, LOVE ONE
ANOTHER. .

85. At this day no Christians will maintain that the
laws of Moses are any longer obligatory upon them;
and yet Jesus has not expressly made any declaration to
that effect. He obeyed them all strictly, with the ex-
ception of that law relating to the Sabbath which he
took various opportunities of violating; and most absurdly, this is the only part of the ceremonial, or not
strictly moral law, which is now attempted to be retained
by the modern Pharisees. His doctrine was so equivocal respecting the old law, that the Apostles themselves
did not understand it, even after they had received the
Holy Spirit. For we find the inspired Peter defending
the old Jewish law at Antioch; and this must have been
many years after the death of Jesus; because the Apostles
remained at Jerusalem some years before they separated
on their missions to the Gentiles, if the early fathers
are to be believed, twelve years.

86. If there be yet any persons who believe that the
Sabbath was not abolished by Jesus Christ, they are

requested to observe, that they are bound to keep it as the Jews kept it; they can neither light a fire nor cook meat on the Sabbath; and for the punishment to which they render themselves liable, if they do, they are referred to Numbers xv. 32 — 36, as previously quoted.

32. And while the children of Israel were in the wilderness, they found a man that gathered sticks upon the Sabbath-day.

33. And they that found him gathering sticks brought him unto Moses and Aaron, and unto all the congregation:

34. And they put him in ward, because it was not declared what should be done unto him.

35. And the Lord said unto Moses, The man shall be surely put to death: all the congregation shall stone him with stones without the camp.

36. And all the congregation brought him without the camp, and stoned him with stones, and he died; as the Lord commanded Moses.

HORÆ SABBATICÆ.

PART II.

HORÆ SABBATICÆ.

PART II.

FROM the following verse in the second chapter of Genesis: 'And God blessed the seventh day, and sanctified it; because that in it he had rested from all the work which God created and made.'

2. Many persons have maintained, that the Sabbath was instituted at the creation, and therefore that it is binding on all mankind, and not confined to the Jews. This would seem a fair inference, if the contrary were not expressly declared; and therefore the book of Genesis must be considered to have been written, by Moses writing the account two thousand five hundred years after the event, proleptically.* And it is a very strong circumstance in favor of this, that it cannot be shown from the sacred books, that any one of the Patriarchs before the flood, or after it, ever kept a Sabbath, or that it ever was kept, until ordered by Moses on the journey of the Israelites from Egypt to Sinai. If the first Patriarchs had kept it, in the history of more than two thousand

* Paley's Moral Philosophy.

five hundred years, from Adam to Moses, it must have been noticed or alluded to. The lives and domestic transactions of Noah and his family, of Abraham, Isaac, Jacob, and Joseph, are very particularly described; but not a single word is ever said of their keeping a Sabbath, or censure upon them for neglecting it, or permission for them in Egypt, or elsewhere, to dispense with it. Upon the meaning of the above passage of Genesis, the Rev. Dr. Paley says:

'Although the blessing and sanctification, *i. e.* the religious distinction and appropriation of that day, was not actually made till many ages afterwards. The words do not assert, that God *then* 'blessed' and 'sanctified' the seventh day; but that he blessed and sanctified it *for that reason:* and if any ask, why the Sabbath, or sanctification of the seventh day, was then mentioned, if it was not *then* appointed, the answer is at hand; the order of connection, and not of time, introduced the mention of the Sabbath, in the history of the subject which it was ordained to commemorate.'

3. When the author of Genesis was giving an account of the orders of God to Adam to erect a tabernacle, or place of worship, to the east of Eden—to Cain and Abel to offer sacrifice—to Noah also to sacrifice when coming out of the ark, and to the latter to abstain from eating blood, &c.; and when he was describing the institution of circumcision, and the paying of tithes by Abraham, he would certainly have said something respecting the Sabbath if it had been then instituted. For of all the rites and ceremonies, there was not one of any thing like the importance of this to the inhabitants of the world, either before or after the flood.

4. An attempt has been made to remove the objection which arises from the omission of any notice of the Sabbath, by the writer of the Pentateuch, before the time of Moses, by observing that the very notoriety of a custom may be the reason why it is never named : and as an example of this kind, the circumstance of circumcision never having been named, from the settlement of the Israelites in Canaan down to the circumcision of Jesus Christ, has been produced. But this argument, the whole of the seventeenth chapter of Genesis completely refutes. All the circumstances there detailed, evidently show that it had not been commonly used before that time. If the observance of the Sabbath had been a common thing, like the observance of circumcision, it would have been named without further notice, as circumcision is named when Jesus was circumcised. The difference in the treatment of the two cases is decisively in favor of the author's argument. When the circumcision of Jesus is named, the history of circumcision is not given as the history of the Sabbath is given in Exodus. If circumcision had been then first instituted, its history would have been given. And the reason why it was not named in the interval alluded to was this, that there was no occasion for it, as it was universally practised during all that time, both by Jews and the *other nations.* The reason why the Sabbath was not named as being kept by the Patriarchs was, because it was not kept by them, and they knew nothing about it.

5. Archbishop Magee says, note 57, on the Doc. of At. : "But in what way is the divine appointment of the

Sabbath recorded? Is it any where asserted by Moses, that God had ordered Adam and his posterity to dedicate every seventh day to holy uses, and to the worship of his name; or that they ever did so, in observance of any such command? No such thing. It is merely said, that having rested from the work of creation, *God blessed the seventh day*, and sanctified it. Now, so far is this passage from being universally admitted to imply a command for the sacred observance of the Sabbath, that some have altogether denied the Sabbath to have been instituted by divine appointment: and the Fathers in general, and especially Justin Martyr, have been considered as totally rejecting the notion of a patriarchal Sabbath. But although, especially after the very able and learned investigation of this subject by Dr. Kennicot in the second of his two dissertations, no doubt can reasonably be entertained of the import of this passage, as relating the divine institution of the Sabbath, yet still the rapidity of the historian has left this rather as matter of inference: and it is certain, that he has no where made *express* mention of the observance of a Sabbath, until the time of Moses.''

6. Mr. Beausobre, in his Introduction to the New Testament, expressly allows, and gives his reasons for believing, that the Sabbath was not instituted till the time of Moses. He admits also, that when it was instituted, it was a festival, not a fast; and he points out the circumstance of Jesus going to a feast on that day, Luke xiv. 1. He asserts that it was given as a sign of the covenant; and was limited to one people, the Jews. He

shows that the conduct of Jesus on the Sabbath places it on the same footing as the other Jewish ceremonies. He allows, that in Genesis the sanctifying the Sabbath-day was spoken by way of anticipation. He says, feastings and rejoicings were also thought essential to the Sabbath, according to Philo, Josephus, and the Thalmudists.— Beaus. Int. Part i. p. 193, &c.* He further says,

'The account of the creation was not given till after the coming of the children of Israel out of Egypt, with a design to turn them from idolatry and the worshipping of creatures. Moses takes from thence an occasion of giving them to understand, that this is the reason why God hath sanctified the seventh day, and appointed this festival, to be by them celebrated every week. Upon this supposition, the sanctifying of the Sabbath does not relate to the creation of the world, where we find it mentioned, but to after ages.—*Ibid.*

7. If the expression in the second chapter of Genesis had been understood by Moses or any of the Prophets to be applicable to all mankind, when they were reproaching the Gentiles for their sins in innumerable instances, and enumerating their offences seriatim, (to warn the Israelites against them,) they would some time or other have reproached them for their neglect of the Sabbath. The Bible is almost filled with the reproachings of the Israelites for their imitations of the vices of the Gentiles, and for their neglect of the Sabbath: but in no one instance is it ever hinted, that the neglect of the Sabbath was one of these examples of imitation. It also is quite

* This book is peculiarly used as a lecture book, by the University of Cambridge, and therefore it is fair to conclude, that this learned body, in which several of our most learned bishops are included, has no objection to its doctrines.

incredible, that the *Gentiles* should not have been even once reproached, for the neglect of this very important rite, if it had been considered applicable to them ; and if it were not applicable to them, it evidently cannot be applicable to us.

8. We will now proceed to examine the passages in the Old Testament relating to this subject.

9. In the sixteenth chapter of Exodus the Sabbath is first instituted ; as it is said in the fourth verse, in order that the Lord might know whether the Israelites would walk in his way or not. And in the fifth verse it is said, that twice as much manna was sent on the sixth day as on other days. In the twenty-second and twenty-third verses, the rulers come to Moses for an explanation of the reason of the double quantity coming on the sixth day ; and then Moses explains to them that the seventh day is to be a Sabbath, or day of rest ; but he there gives them no reason why the seventh day was fixed on, rather than the sixth or any other day ; and in this chapter it is merely stated to be ordered to try them if they would walk in the way of the Lord or not.

22. And it came to pass, that on the sixth day they gathered twice as much bread, two omers for one man : and all the rulers of the congregation came and told Moses.

23. And he said unto them, This is that which the Lord hath said, To-morrow is the rest of the holy Sabbath unto the Lord : bake that which ye will bake to-day, and seethe that ye will seethe ; and that which remaineth over lay up for you to be kept until the morning.

24. And they laid it up till the morning, as Moses bade ; and it did not stink, neither was there any worm therein.

25. And Moses said, Eat that to-day ; for to-day is a Sabbath unto the Lord : to-day ye shall not find it in the field.

26. Six days ye shall gather it ; but on the seventh day, which is the Sabbath, in it there shall be none.

27. And it came to pass, that there went out some of the people on the seventh day for to gather, and they found none.

28. And the Lord said unto Moses, How long refuse ye to keep my commandments and my laws?

29. See, for that the Lord hath given you the Sabbath, therefore he giveth you on the sixth day the bread of two days: abide ye every man in his place ; let no man go out of his place on the seventh day.

30. So the people rested on the seventh day.

10. In several places of the quotation above, a mistranslation has taken place ; the definite or emphatic article has been used instead of the indefinite one. Thus, in the twenty-third verse it is said, *the* rest of *the* holy Sabbath, instead of *a* rest of *a* holy Sabbath. Again, in the twenty-sixth verse it ought to have been said, on the seventh day, which is *a* Sabbath, in it, &c., not *the* Sabbath, &c.

11. In the twenty-ninth verse the emphatic or definite article is correctly· used, *the* Sabbath, according to the Hebrew text, the Sabbath being there spoken of as instituted. The author has been the more particular in the examination of these texts, because he has met with several clergymen, not learned in the Hebrew language, who have maintained, that from the use of the emphatic article in the places in question, a previous establishment, and an existence of the Sabbath must be necessarily inferred. But the fact is, that the contrary infer-

ence must be drawn from the Hebrew text: and no
Hebrew scholar will doubt a moment on the correctness
of what is said respecting the Hebrew definite article.
It is not one of the points of this language about which
there has been   ̣y dispute.

12. If this related merely to the common affairs of life,
no one would doubt that the coming of the rulers̃ of the
congregation to Moses showed clearly that they were
ignorant of the Sabbath — that they had never heard of
such a thing before : for if they had known that it was
unlawful to provide food, or gather sticks to light a fire
to cook it, or to do any other act of work or labor, how
could they have had any doubt what the double quantity
was sent for on the day before the Sabbath? And the
answer given by Moses in the next verse, This is what
the Lord hath said, implies that the information given
to them was new. If the practice of keeping the Sabbath had prevailed with the Israelites when in Egypt in
their bondage, (a thing very unlikely,) or if it had been
known to them that it was their duty to keep it when in
their power, the book would simply have told us, that
they gathered twice as much on the sixth day, because
the next was the Sabbath ; there would have been no
coming together of the elders, or of speech-making by
Moses. Besides, the text says, that it was ordered here
to try them, whether they would walk in the way of
Jehovah at this particular time or not. This is directly
contrary to the idea of its being an established ordinance
from the creation. It was here given as a test of their
obedience — it was continued afterwards, as a sign of the

covenant entered into betwixt God and them. Nor is there any where an intimation, that the appointment of the Sabbath was the renewal of an ancient institutiðn, which had been neglected, forgotten, or suspended.

13. In the Decalogue which is ordained in the twentieth chapter of Exodus, the Sabbath is first given in all its plenitude; but it is with the remainder of the Decalogue expressly limited to the children of Israel. God begins with saying, I am the Lord *thy** God, which have brought *thee* out of the land of Egypt, out of the house of bondage. Here he calls the Israelites *thee;* and he goes on throughout the whole addressing them in the second person singular, *Thou* shalt have no other Gods but me, &c. If the language is to bear its common and usual signification, the law as here given is limited to the Israelites. Upon the meaning of this passage may be applied, the very excellent rule of criticism laid down by Bishop Horsley in his controversy with Dr. Priestley.

'It is a principle with me, that the true sense of any phrase in the New Testament is what may be called its standing sense, that which will be the first to occur to common people of every country and in every age.'—Horsley to Priestley, p. 23; Priestley's Letters to Horsley, p. 289.

14. In the twentieth chapter of Exodus, at the tenth verse, the emphatic or definite article has been substituted for the indefinite one, the same as has been done in the sixteenth chapter, as was before shown.

*The pronoun is here very correctly translated from the Hebrew: it is precisely as it is in English. Not, the Lord God, as he is usually called, but, *the Lord* THY *God.* But it would have been still more correct to have said, *Jehovah thy God*, instead of. *the Lord thy God.*

15. In this place, where it means to describe that the seventh day is to be a day of rest, it says, *a* Sabbath : but where it has reference to what had passed before, viz. to its previous institution, it says, *the* Sabbath. This is all consistent with the arguments of the gentlemen before referred to. When the text is correctly translated, their arguments are in fact decisively against themselves.*

16. Again, the Sabbath is ordained, in the thirty-first chapter of Exodus and fourteenth verse; and it is here again expressly limited to the children of Israel, and declared to be for a sign of the covenant. God says, it is holy *unto you*, not unto all the world. Again, he says,

Wherefore the children of Israel (not all mankind) shall keep, &c., for a perpetual covenant, &c. It is a sign betwixt me and the children of Israel for ever.

17. How can more clear words of limitation be used? And Dr. Paley says,

'It does not seem easy to understand how the Sabbath could be a *sign* between God and the people of Israel, unless the observance of it was peculiar to that people, and designed to be so.'

---

*The Hebrew is remarkable for its brevity, and words are often obliged to be inserted to make sense in our language; in almost innumerable places the helping verb is obliged to be added. Thus in the tenth verse it is said, *but the seventh day is.* There is no authority in the Hebrew for the word *is.* The literal translation of the words is, *but the seventh day a Sabbath* The helping verb is here evidently wanting; and it must be discovered from the context what part of the verb must be used. It is submitted to the Hebrew scholar, whether it would not be perfectly justifiable in this case to use the words will be, or shall be? and write, But the seventh day shall be a (day of rest) Sabbath. This would strengthen the argument. It is not of any consequence. But no one could say it was mistranslated, if it said, The seventh day *shall be* a Sabbath.

13. Speak thou also unto the children of Israel, saying, Verily my Sabbaths ye shall keep : for it is a sign between me and you throughout your generations; that ye may know that I am the Lord that doth sanctify you.

14. Ye shall keep the Sabbath therefore ; for it is holy unto you : every one that defileth it shall surely be put to death : for whosoever doeth any work therein, that soul shall be cut off from among his people.

15. Six days may work be done ; but in the seventh is the Sabbath holy to the Lord : whosoever doeth any work in the Sabbath-day, he shall surely be put to death.

16. Wherefore the children of Israel shall keep the Sabbath, to observe the Sabbath throughout their generations, for a perpetual covenant.

17. It is a sign between me and the children of Israel for ever : for in six days the Lord made heaven and earth, and on the seventh day he rested, and was refreshed.

18. In the fourteenth verse God does not say that it is *holy*, but it is *holy unto you*. A clear limitation to the children of Israel.

Exod. xxxiv. 28.— And he was there with the Lord forty days and forty nights ; he did neither eat bread nor drink water. And he wrote upon the tables the words of *the covenant*, the ten commandments.

19. How, after reading these passages, can any one deny, that the Decalogue was given as a sign of the covenant betwixt God and the Israelites ? and it seems to follow, that when the covenant was fulfilled, the sign was abolished.

20. Upon the reason assigned in Exodus for the institution of the Sabbath, Dr. Paley justly observes :

" It may be remarked, that although in Exodus the commandment is founded upon God's rest from the creation, in

Deuteronomy the commandment is repeated with a reference
to a different event. 'Six days shalt thou labour, and do
all thy work; but the seventh day is the Sabbath of the Lord
thy God; in it thou shalt not do any work, thou, nor thy son,
nor thy daughter, nor thy man-servant, nor thy maid-servant,
nor thine ox, nor thine ass, nor any of thy cattle, nor the
stranger that is within thy gates; that thy man-servant and
thy maid-servant may rest as well as thou. And remember
thou wast servant in the land of Egypt, and that the Lord thy
God brought thee out thence, through a mighty hand, and by
a stretched-out arm : *therefore* the Lord thy God commanded
thee to keep the Sabbath-day.' It is farther observable, that
God's rest from the creation is proposed as the reason of the
institution, even where the institution itself is spoken of as
peculiar to the Jews. 'Wherefore the children of Israel shall
keep the Sabbath, to observe the Sabbath throughout their
generations, for a perpetual covenant. *It is a sign between me*
and the children of Israel for ever: *for* in six days the Lord
made heaven and earth, on the seventh day he rested, and
was refreshed.' ''

21. In the following places the order to keep the Sabbath is repeated; but in every one it is limited to the
Israelites: Exod. xxxv. 2, 3. Lev. xxiii. 3, 15. xxv.

22. The limitation of the Sabbath to the children of
Israel, and the making it a sign of the covenant betwixt
God and them, expressly negatives the construction put
upon the expression in Genesis, that by it the Sabbath
was instituted. It is making God act most absurdly, to
make him first institute the Sabbath for the whole
world, and then give it as a sign limited to the Israelites,
when, from its being previously established, it could
most clearly be no such thing.

23. From several of these passages we see that the
Sabbath was ordained as a sign of the covenant, made

betwixt God and the Israelites. To be a sign was the reason of a Sabbath being instituted, not the resting of God from his work: though the selection of the seventh, instead of the third or fourth or other day of the week, was made to remind the Israelites of that event. As we have seen in Exodus, that it was given as a sign of the covenant, so it was understood by Ezekiel, who.says,

10. Wherefore I caused 'them to go forth out of the land of Egypt, and brought them into the wilderness:

11. And I gave them my statutes, and showed them my judgments, which, if a man do, he shall even live in them.

12. Moreover also, I gave them my Sabbaths, to be a sign between me and them, that they might know that I am the Lord that sanctified them.— Ezek. xx. 10 – 12.

24. On this Dr. Paley says: Here the Sabbath is plainly spoken of as *given;* and what else can that mean, but as *first instituted* in the wilderness?

25. The Prophet Nehemiah also expressly declares, that the Sabbath was first made known to them, or instituted on their exod from Egypt. He says, ix. 13.

13. Thou camest down also upon Mount Sinai, and spakest with them from heaven, and gavest them right judgments, and true laws, good statutes and commandments:

14. And madest known unto them, thy holy Sabbath, and commandest them precepts, &c.

26. How could it be said that he made known to them the Sabbath there, if it were known to them before? The language of Scripture must not be so wrested, from its plain obvious signification, to gratify prejudice, or serve particular theories.

27. When God fixed the seventh day for the Sabbath with Moses, he chose the seventh to commemorate the finishing of the creation. In the same way afterward we shall find that, when Constantine wished to fix upon one day, to be set apart for divine worship, he chose the first to commemorate the day of the resurrection. But neither the Sabbath nor the Sunday as a holy day was established till long after the events, in honor of which they were fixed upon, had been passed.

28. But the observance of the seventh day of the week as a Sabbath, is only a small part of the Sabbatical law.*

---

* It is curious to observe how some persons can make difficulties in dispensing with the words of the law, when thereby they gratify their passions, their prejudices, or their interest; and how easily in other cases they can dispense with them, or, rather say, set them at defiance. They say, the law of the Sabbath cannot be abolished, because it was given by God before the Israelites existed, and therefore is binding on all mankind, and not on the Israelites only. If this argument be good in one case, it is good in every other similar case. In the fourth verse of the ninth chapter of Genesis, it is said,

4. But flesh with the life thereof, which is the blood thereof, shall ye not eat. This was said to Noah.

This is confirmed in the seventeenth chapter of Leviticus, where it is said,

10. And whatsoever man there be of the house of Israel, or *of the strangers* that sojourn among you, that eateth any manner of blood, I will even set my face against that soul that eateth blood, and will cut him off from among his people.

In the following verses, to the end of the fifteenth, this order is several times repeated, *including strangers;* and in Deuteronomy xii. 16, it is again repeated.

16. Only ye shall not eat the blood; ye shall pour it out upon the earth as water.

And in Acts, when all the other laws of Moses are expressly abolished, this is excepted by name. And yet Christians of every denomination eat blood and animals strangled every day.

What does all this prove? It proves that, generally, reason has nothing to do with religion. And that men are of that religion, which their priest and their nurse happen accidentally to profess. This observation will offend many persons; but it is, notwithstanding, perfectly true.

In the twenty-fifth chapter of Leviticus a Sabbatical year is ordained: how absurd to take one part of the law relating to Sabbaths and not the other! If a Sabbath be kept because it is ordained by God; consistently, one Sabbath must be kept as well as the other.

29. The Sabbath, we have seen, was given as a sign of a covenant betwixt God and the Jews, which covenant was expressly abolished by the coming of Jesus Christ; then it necessarily follows, that the sign of the covenant should no longer be observed.

30. If a Sabbath be kept, because it was ordained by God previously to the time of Jesus, it must be kept as he ordained it; and how he ordained it we can only know from the books and the practice of the Jews.

31. They were to do no work on that day, not even to light a fire; no victuals could be dressed, or even put on or taken off the table on that day: the candle was lighted before the day began; and if it went out, it could not be lighted again; and if a draught of water was wanted, it could not be fetched.

32. It has been observed to me, that it appears from Acts xiii. 42. xvi. 13. xviii. 4. that the primitive Christians did not relax in their observance of the Sabbath. True; nor did they relax in the observance of any other part of the Jewish law for some years. They certainly kept the Sabbath until it, with all other Jewish rites, was declared to be abolished by the Apostles assembled at Jerusalem. They might meet on the Sunday, as Christians who are devout at this day have prayers in their houses morning and evening, or fast on Fridays

and Saturdays. They assembled also in the evening to celebrate their love-feasts, and again to sing hymns before day-light. If these times were not chosen in order that the day might be given to worldly duties; pray let any divine tell what they were selected for?

33. It cannot be said that they assembled at those times to avoid persecution ; for they must then all have been in the state of "lapsed;" that is, of those who had denied their Saviour, or refused the honors of martyrdom, and were therefore excommunicated. It is well known that a great feud arose in the church, respecting the read-mission into it of those who had withdrawn from perse-cution. Some refusing to admit them on any terms ; and others being willing to receive them again after severe penance. So far from attempting to avoid the honors of martyrdom, by secreting themselves ; it is well known that these honors were sought for by Christians with eagerness :—Vid. Pliny's Letters to Trajan. It has been said that they fled to the catacombs to conceal the rites of their religion, and to avoid persecution. This surely was a most dangerous expedient; for as there was only one road into them, by closing it, their enemies might have destroyed them with the greatest facility.

34. The truth of the matter was this—they frequented the catacombs to celebrate there the services to the dead ; as they were afterward celebrated in the crypts under the choirs of our ancient cathedrals : for which purpose these crypts were beautifully ornamented, as may still be seen in the cathedral at Canterbury. The Council of

Elvira, by one of its canons, forbid the use of candles in the catacombs, in the celebration of the services for the dead ; for this wise reason,

'That they might not disturb the souls of the deceased.'

35. The assembling in the evening and early in the morning, was evidently done to leave to slaves, servants, tradesmen, and all others, the means of pursuing their usual avocations during the remainder of the day.

36. If it be clearly shown, by quotations and fair argument, that the Sabbath was abolished by the New Testament, it is not of much consequence, what the persons called the Fathers of the church say upon the subject; or what was their practice : we have as much right to judge for ourselves as they had. But it may be said, that they may have adopted a practice from the Apostles, as they lived so near them. Then we will enquire what was their practice and opinions.

37. The works of the apostolic fathers, the apostolical constitutions, and indeed all the works of the ancient fathers of the church before Justin Martyr, are allowed, by the first divines and bishops of the present day, to be forgeries; therefore, though their works contain passages favorable to the argument, they will not be used.

38. It cannot be denied, that Justin Martyr must have known perfectly well, what was the doctrine of the early Christians upon this subject. He is the very first of the Christian fathers of whom we have any entire works, whose genuineness is not disputed. In his dialogue with Trypho the Jew, he says :

'The new law will have you keep a perpetual Sabbath; and you, when you have passed one day in idleness, think you are religious, not knowing why that was commanded you. The Lord our God is not pleased with such things as these. If any among you is guilty of perjury or fraud, let him cease from these crimes; if he is an adulterer, let him repent, and he will have kept the kind of Sabbath pleasing to God.' Again :—'Do you see that the elements are never idle nor keep a Sabbath? Continue as you were created. For if there was no need of circumcision before Abraham, nor of the observation of the *Sabbaths*, and *festivals*, and oblations before Moses, neither now likewise is there any need of them after Jesus Christ, &c. Tell me why did not God teach those to perform such things, who preceded Moses and Abraham, just men, of great renown, and who were well-pleasing to him, though they neither were circumcised nor observed Sabbaths?' Again :— 'As therefore circumcision *began* from Abraham, and the *Sabbath*, sacrifices, and oblations *from Moses;* which it has been shown were ordained on account of your nation's hardness of heart, so, according to the council of the fathers, they were to end in Jesus Christ the Son of God.'

39. Similar passages might be selected from Irenæus and Tertullian, intending to prove that the Sabbath was a special ordinance confined to the Jews, as a sign of a covenant betwixt God and them.

40. That the Christians assembled on the Sunday in the time of Justin Martyr, one hundred and fifty years after the birth of Jesus, for the purpose of divine worship, cannot be denied, if it were desired so to do, as the following curious passage proves. But it was not compulsory, nor esteemed a sin to neglect it, or do any ordinary business on that day.

41. The following is a copy of Section 89, of Justin's Apology :

'Upon Sunday we all assemble, that being the first day in which God set himself to work upon the dark void, in order to make the world, and in which Jesus Christ our Saviour rose again from the dead: for the day before Saturday, he was crucified; and the day after, which is Sunday, he appeared to his Apostles and disciples, and taught them what I have now proposed to your consideration.'

42. It is a curious circumstance, that the Christians, according to Justin, did not keep the Sunday, because God had ended his work, but because he had begun it, on that day.

43. In the passage here cited, Justin is giving the reasons why the Christians observed the Sunday. He was one of the most celebrated of the early Christian martyrs. We are told that he was a heathen philosopher, converted to Christianity. This passage is from a well-known apology, written in order to convert the Emperor Antoninus Pius. It is not possible to believe, that if the observance of Sunday had been of divine or apostolical appointment, he would not here have stated it. In other parts of his works he quotes the authority of the Apostles for the doctrines which he teaches. If it had been considered by the Christians in his day as a divine ordinance, in lieu of the old Sabbath, we should here most certainly have been informed of it. It was evidently a municipal or fiscal regulation, a part of their discipline established by themselves, and nothing more; and his authority, the best and earliest in the Christian church, decides the question beyond dispute.

44. The earliest of the Christians, who kept the Sunday, always kept it as a festival with joy and glad-

ness, to celebrate the glorious resurrection of their
Saviour. Tertullian declares it unlawful to fast on a
Sunday, *or to worship on the knees** on that day. The
sixty-sixth of the apostolical canons declares, that if an
ecclesiastic should fast on a Sunday, he should be
deposed; and if a layman should do it, he should be
excommunicated. Mr. Whiston thought with the Catholics, that these canons were not forgeries: but whether
forgeries or not, they show all they are quoted for;
namely, the opinion of Christians in a very early day.
St. Augustine† condemns fasting on a Sunday, for the
reason given above; namely, because it was a day of joy
and gladness.—Ep. 86. ad Casulan.

45. It may be doubtful what authority the Protestants
of this day may choose to allow to the canons of the
Council of Nice; but as they adopt the Nicene Creed,
they will not deny that they are entitled to some respect
in the decision of the question. Of what was the general
opinion of the Church in their day, in such cases as this
opinion shall be clearly stated by them. The following
is an extract from the 16th canon:

Caput 16. de Adoratione seu Genuflexione.
 . . . . in sanctis dominicis diebus sacrisque aliis solennitatibus
nullæ fiant genuflexiones, quia tota Sancta Ecclesia in hisce
lætatur, et exultat diebus, genuflexiones autem afflictionis
tristitiæ, timoris et mœroris tessara sunt et signum, ideo
omittendæ sunt diebus festis, ac maxime die resurrectionis
Domini nostri Jesu Christi a mortuis. Hoc autem caput sine

---

*Die dominica jejunare nefas ducimus, vel *de genicolis adorare*.
Tertul. De Cor. cap. 3.

† Called by Dr. Lardner, the glory of Africa.

anathemate est. Hist. Philip. Labbei conc. Nic. ad Can. 16.
A. D. 325. Pap. Silvester. 1.

46. In the Sacrosancta Concilia Philip. Labbei et Gabr.
Cossartii, tom. 2. p. 385, the Sabbatarians are placed the
first amongst seventy-seven named sects :

It is said, 'Rerum obliti erant isti Dei vocem per Isaiam
prophetam ita contestantem : Odio habuit anima mea Sabbata
vestra, et neomenias vestras, et facta sunt mihi gravia.'

47. The Manicheans and Marcionites, sects of heretics
to whom the modern Puritans or Evangelical Christians
probably would not like to be compared, kept the Sunday
as a day of humiliation.   This gave great scandal to the
orthodox of that day, and to most, if not all, other
heretics.   Pope Leo the First, in his fifteenth Epistle to
Turibius, says, "The Manicheans have been convicted
in the examination which we have made, of passing the
Sunday, which is consecrated to the resurrection of our
Lord, in mortification and fasting."

48. By a decree of the Council of Gangres in Paphla-
gonia, about the year 357, all those are anathematized
who, from devotion and mortification,* pass the Sunday
in fasting.—See Pagi. Crit. Bar. An. 357 and 360.
Though Protestants may despise the authority of these
ancient Popes and Councils, yet they cannot deny, that
they prove what were the early opinions of the Church,
which is all they are quoted for.

49. God forbid, that the characters of Constantine
and Eusebius should be held up as examples worthy of

* Concil. Gang. Canon. xviii. Διὰ νομιζομένην ἄσκησιν.

imitation ; but yet it cannot be denied, that the edict of
the former, by which the observation of Sunday as a day
of rest was first ordained by law, and made imperative on
Christians, bespeaks in every part of it sound discretion.
His edict says,

‘ Let all judges and towns-people, and the occupations of all
trades, rest on the venerable day of the sun. But let those who
are situated in the country, freely and at full liberty, attend to
the business of agriculture ; because it often happens, that no
other day is so fit for sowing corn, or planting vines, lest the
critical moment being let slip, men should lose the commodities
granted them by the providence of Heaven.’*

50. When Constantine was passing this law, with
Eusebius and the clergy of his newly-established religion to assist and advise him, can it be believed, that
he would not have stated, that it was done in obedience
to the command of God, as handed down by tradition, or
by writing, if such it had been considered? The contrary cannot be believed, whether he be considered as a
hypocrite, or a devotee.

51. Though Dr. Paley considers the Sabbath to be
abolished, he thinks that,

‘ The *assembling* upon the first day of the week for the purpose of public worship and religious instruction, is a law of
Christianity of divine appointment:’

but he goes on to qualify this by adding,

* Omnes judices urbanæque plebes et cunctarum artium officia
venerabili die solis quiescant. Ruri tamen positi agrorum culturæ
libere licenterque inserviant, quoniam frequenter evenit, ut non aptius
alio die frumenta sulcis aut vineæ scrobibus mandentur, ne occasione
momenti pereat commoditas cœlesti provisione concessa. Dat. Nonis
Mart. Crispo 11. et Constantino 11. Conss. Corp. Jur. Civ. Codicis, lib.
3. tit. 12.

'The resting on that day from our employments, longer than we are detained from them by attendance upon these assemblies, is to Christians an ordinance of *human institution*.'

52. Now the question, whether the assembling for public worship on *the Sunday* differently from any other day, be of human or divine appointment, has nothing to do with the appointment of *divine worship generally*, but only to its being fixed to that particular time. His inference is merely drawn from the apparent assembling of the Apostles and disciples on the first day of the week, as described in the three places quoted in the first Part; whence he infers that there must have been some appointment by divine authority unknown to us. This it has been shown that not one of the texts will warrant. Granting, for the sake of argument, that they were assembled all the three times alluded to by previous appointment, and not by accident, and that this was fixed to the first day of the week, the fair inference is, that the fixing of this day was not of divine, but of human invention only: for it cannot be believed, that an ordinance of such great importance would not have been stated to be of divine authority, if it had been so considered. It is quite absurd to suppose afterward, when great and even bloody feuds were taking place, respecting the observance of the Sabbath on the seventh day, that not one of the Fathers or parties should have stated, that the Apostles had established the observance of the Sunday *instead* of it. Nothing could have been more favorable to the anti-sabbatarians; and in no other way can their silence be accounted for, than by the sup-

position, that they did not allege this, because the falsity of their allegation would have been notorious. If the case had been doubtful even, they would have availed themselves of it, as far as was in their power.

53. Some persons have imagined, that the day of the Sun, dies Dominica, the first day of the week, the day peculiarly dedicated to the Sun by the heathens, was called the Lord's-day, out of honor to Jesus Christ. And Dr. Priestley had this idea : he says,

'That before the death of John, it had obtained the epithet of the Lord's-day. As John did nothing more than use the epithet κυριακή, to distinguish the day he alluded to, and wrote for the use of Christians in general, of that and all succeeding ages, it is evident, that he knew they wanted no other mark to discover what day he meant, and that, therefore, it was a name universally given to the first day at that time by Christians.'

54. No doubt he knew that the Christians would understand him, and the Doctor might have added, the heathens also. For it was known by this name before Jesus was born, in honor of the Sun, who was always called Dominus Sol, and the day, dies Dominica. —See Dupuis sur tous les cultes, vol. 3. p. 41. ed. 4to. The Persians called their God Mithra always the Lord Mithra ; but it is well known, that Mithra was nothing but the Sun. Dr. Paley has fallen into the same mistake with Dr. Priestley.

55. The Syrians gave to the Sun the epithet of Adonis, or Lord. Adon is yet the word for Lord in the Welsh Celtic language. Porphyry, in a prayer which he addresses to the Sun, calls him Dominus Sol. And in the

consecration of the seven days of the week to the different planets, the day of the Sun is called the day of the Lord Sol, or dies Dominica; when the others are called only by their names, as dies Martis, &c.—See Porphyry, de Abstinentia, l. 4. Dupuis, v. 3. p. 41—55. ed. 4to. Every one of the ancient nations gave the Sun the epithet of Lord or Master, or some title equivalent to it, as Κύριος in Greek, Dominus in Latin. As the Sun was called Dominus, the Moon or Isis was called Domina. On the side of a church in Bologna, formerly a temple, the following inscription still remains: Dominæ Isidi Victrici.

56. The multiplication, by the laws of society, of artificial offences, which are in themselves no crimes, such as those created by the excise laws, and the prohibition of innocent amusements on the Sunday, have a very strong tendency to corrupt the public morals.

57. To convert an act pleasurable and agreeable to the youthful mind, and innocent in its own nature, such as a game of cricket, on a Sunday evening, into a crime, is to treat the Lord's-prayer with contempt. It is to lead into temptation the uncorrupted; who, by the nature of their youth, are the most open to it. Another objection arises, from the circumstance that the laboring orders of mankind, who are obliged to work all the six days of the week to earn their subsistence, are consequently much more exposed to temptation than the higher orders, to whom every day is a Sabbath, or day of rest; and who increase the temptation to the others to break it, by

breaking it with impunity themselves whenever they think proper.

58. The temptation is also much greater to the laborer, who works all the other six days, than to the rich man, to whom they are all Sabbaths or days of rest. The rich man, who has never worked, can scarcely form an idea of the pleasure of the Sabbath to the poor laborer.

59. In sermons, and in books of different kinds, put into the hands of young and ignorant persons, Sabbath-breaking is constantly held up as a most heinous and terrible sin; and when persons thus taught to consider it as a sin of magnitude, equal to the commission of real crimes, are once tempted to a commission of the offence, they become hardened. An effect is produced upon their minds, very different from what it would be if they were merely told that Sabbath-breaking was wrong, because it was a breach of a municipal regulation, of little conse-quence: and that if they persisted in it, they should be made to pay the penalty of the law, *three shillings and fourpence.*

60. It is the very acmé of impolicy, and has the strongest tendency to corrupt the morals of a people, to teach them that trifling offences, which from any peculiar circumstance they are constantly exposed to daily and almost insuperable temptation to commit, are of a heinous nature. The mind by repeatedly commit-ting a minor offence, colored to it as an atrocious act, becomes hardened and prepared by a species of appren-ticeship for the commission of the worst crimes. Hence it is we constantly find culprits at the gallows charging

the sin of Sabbath-breaking, as they call it, with the origin of their abandoned course of life; and there can be no doubt that they are correct in so doing.—By considering the Sabbath or day of rest in the point of view in which it has been placed, merely as a municipal regulation, it is evident that the occasional breach of it will not be attended with the same pernicious consequences as attend the breach of it when considered as a divine ordinance. The persons who sincerely appropriate the whole day to the observance of religious duties, no doubt will be more pious than those who appropriate only part of it: as those are more pious, who pray morning and night, than those who pray once a day. But the minds of those who, either by business or pleasure, are induced to neglect it, will not be hardened in vice : and a person of good common sense will know, that if he perform the duties of prayer and thanksgiving on some other day, when he has been induced to neglect them on the day fixed by the law of the land, the offence, further than merely the breach of a trifling municipal regulation, valued at 3s. 4d., will be in a great measure atoned for.

61. If the Sunday be considered as a divinely appointed substitute for the Jewish Sabbath, the consequence follows, that it must, or at least ought, if consistency be attended to, to be kept in every respect as the Jewish Sabbath was ordained to be kept. In the multifarious and complicated concerns of a great commercial nation, it is not possible to keep it as strictly as ordained by the letter of the old law. Hence it must be violated every day, both by governments and individuals. In conse-

quence of considering this institution of divine appointment, many persons of the best dispositions are placed almost daily in situations the most painful. The distressing nature of these situations evidently proceeds from the mistaken idea that it is of divine, and not of human, appointment. If it be the former, it evidently admits of no modification : but if it be only the latter, it as evidently may be varied, or even dispensed with, as circumstances require. Being ordained to be kept by the magistrate, it is wrong not to keep it; but the offence in the former case is far greater than in the latter.

62. In the neighborhood of the author, an honest, respectable, industrious man lived at an inn as hostler, and after some time his master obtained a share in a mail coach, and he had the horses to prepare and take care of. It is evident that this man must break the Sabbath every Sunday, or abandon the situation by which he maintained his family in comfort ; a situation for which he was much better qualified than for any other. He applied to the author for advice, having read his Bible, and wishing to do his duty; but not wishing to ruin himself, and send his wife and children to the parish. He was recommended to go to his parish priest. What passed is unknown to the author, except that he returned with a perfect contempt for the wretched sophistry of his ghostly adviser, who happened to be one of the *Evangelical* Christians, as they call themselves. He was a man of strong common sense ; it was not likely that he should do otherwise.

63. Very good men amongst both the French and English have wished the observance of the Sunday to be abolished. But surely they have reasoned very incorrectly. Some have said that it is unwise to lose one seventh part of the labor of the industrious classes of mankind, and that on this account it would conduce greatly to the riches of a state to abolish it. This is the argument of the West India planter, and no doubt is true. It is the reason why postmasters never wish to have their horses stand still in the stable ; and no doubt it is true : but it requires no comment.

64. Others have said, it is a great hardship, to deprive a poor man of the produce of the seventh part of his voluntary labor, for the support of his family. This is no doubt true also, if the argument be applied to one family only; but if it be applied to a whole nation, nothing can be more untrue. And nothing is more easy than to show, that if in a whole nation the observance of Sunday were to be abolished, though the rich would be greatly benefited, no poor man would be bettered in point of pecuniary concerns to the amount of a single farthing, and in many respects the comforts and enjoyments of the poor would be very greatly abridged.* Some persons have maintained that a day of rest is a day of idleness and dissipation, alike destructive to the purses and the morals of the industrious part of the community. This is to reason against the use, from the abuse of a thing. It only shows the necessity of proper

* See Edinburgh Review, No. LXVII. p. 23.

regulations. A person may as well argue against the planting of vines or barley, because people get drunk.

65. As a human ordinance, nothing can be more wise than the observance of a periodical day of devotion, rest, and recreation; but, as a Sabbath, in the strict sense of the Jews and Calvinists, nothing can be well more pernicious. The practice of the Roman Catholics seems to be not only the most consistent with Scripture, but the most rational. After their devotions are over, they have no scruple to join in any innocent recreation and amusement. How different this is to the conduct of our modern Pharisees! Many persons will not on any account read a newspaper on a Sunday, or allow a little music in their house on that day on any consideration. An instance is known to the author, where a Scotchman informed a young man, visiting at his house, that it was not usual with them to laugh on the Lord's day, and he hoped he would abstain from it. All this arises from the mistaken idea, that the observance of the Lord's day is a renewal of the Jewish Sabbath.

66. The author feels a pleasure in stating, that the old law of England, before its late corruption by the modern Pharisees, was perfectly accordant with his view of the subject. The Sunday is classed amongst the *festivals*, not the fasts. All *works* of necessity were permitted, and only such as were not necessary were forbidden; vid. Act of Charles 2d, c. 2. s. 7: and by King James's Book of Sports, such amusements were allowed as at that time were thought necessary and innocent; such as DANCING, archery, leaping, vaulting,

May Games, Whitson ales, morris dances, a species of dramatic entertainment, &c.: vid. Dalton, c. 46. It is very much to be desired that they were re-enacted, that the people might be encouraged after divine service to apply to cheerful amusements, instead of the ale-house, or what is as bad, the petty conventicles of morose Calvinistic fanatics,* who fancy they have a call to preach up, what in their hands is nothing better than a *prava immodica et exitiabilis superstitio,*† to their gaping auditors, almost as ignorant as themselves, for which there is no remedy but silent contempt.

67. The following injunctions were published by Queen Elizabeth and Edward the Sixth; and as no doubt they speak the opinions of the leading reformers of that day, they are curious, and deserving of respect.

'All parsons, vicars and curates shall teach and declare unto the people, that they may with a safe and quiet conscience, after their common prayer in time of harvest, labor upon the holy and festival days, and save that thing which God hath sent. And if for any scrupulosity or grudge of conscience they shall abstain from working upon those days, that then they shall grievously offend and displease God.'

68. It is necessary to observe that festival days, according to act of parliament, include all Sundays. It is a thing very much to be desired, that the generality of persons engaged in business would be content with the

---

* Calvin, the founder of the doctrine of these people, who burnt Servetus for differing in opinion with him, declared he believed in what he taught, *quia incredibile est, because it is incredible.* He was quite right; it is the only ground on which it can be believed, because it is contrary to the moral attributes of God.

† Pliny, Tacitus, Suetonius.

religion of their ancestors, at least until they can produce some good reasons for making a change ; leaving
the task of expounding difficult texts of the Bible to the
divines and polemics.

69. A learned traveller, speaking of France, says,

"Methodists and enthusiasts there are none; and nothing
more astonishes a Frenchman than to describe the ascendancy
of Methodism in England, the death-like gloom of an English
Sunday, and the vagaries of the jumpers and other such
fanatics, who disgrace the intelligence of the British people.
It was repeated to me at least fifty times in reply to my observations—'though men are forbidden to work on a Sunday,
they are not forbidden to play;' 'and if,' said a French priest
to me, 'you would keep Sunday out of respect to our Lord's
ascension, instead of keeping the Sabbath, surely that ascension
is a subject rather of gaiety than sadness."

70. When a Frenchman has performed the devotional
exercises required by his religion, he does not think
there is any thing wrong in doing such occasional labor
or work on a Sunday, as may offer itself or be required.
He does not consider that he is acting against the word
of God ; he is only giving up part of his own enjoyment,
the recreation which is allowed to him : and if he have
a family, he thinks he is making a meritorious sacrifice,
rather than otherwise. And this is perfectly consistent
with the idea of it, as a day of festivity ordained by the
church.

71. It has been said that Jesus wept, but never
laughed ; but for all this, he had no objection to cheerful society, and that to a pretty liberal extent, or he
would not by a miracle, at Cana in Galilee, have pro-

vided more wine, when the guests had already taken as much as the host had thought proper to provide for them. Nor would he have attended a feast on the Sabbath-day, as described in Luke xiv.

72. The people of Geneva appear to keep the Sunday more correctly than any other persons. During divine service all the wine-houses, shops, &c., are closed, and the gates of the town opened to none but surgeons and accoucheurs, except some very urgent case is made out to the satisfaction of the magistrate. The labors of husbandry are permitted in harvest, and at other times, when the magistrate gives permission for them, and thinks it proper. After the day's devotion is over, the evening is spent at dramatic entertainments, or in visiting, dancing, playing at athletic games, such as football, &c.

73. It is constantly the boast of Christians, that their religion is a religion of cheerfulness, in opposition to objectors, who have charged it with being the contrary. Surely the objection must be considerably strengthened by the conversion of fifty-two days (one-seventh of the whole year) from days of festivity into days of mourning and sadness. Though the fanatic may approve this conversion, the philosophic Christian, the real philanthropist, must view it with sorrow and regret.

74. Thus, when the day is considered as it ought to be, merely as a human ordinance, it can be regulated without difficulty, by the governors of states, as is most suitable to times and circumstances. But if it be considered as a divine command, it is evidently out of their

reach or control. However pernicious an effect may arise, they have no means to obviate it, without what ought never to be seen—the government intentionally violating the laws which it tells its people are sacred, and cannot be violated without the commission of a great sin.—The governors despatching mail-coaches in all directions, and fining poor men for being shaved before they go to church, on a Sunday morning.*

75. It will now probably be demanded, whether a wish is entertained to abolish the observance of the Sunday or not: to which the reply is, certainly not. The Jewish Sabbath was abolished by Jesus; and if it were in the power of the Author, it should not be restored by him. But the question is not about the seventh day of the week, but about the Sunday, the first; and concerning the latter, the question is, not whether it is to be abolished, but whether it is to be kept, subject to the regulation of the government, as a fast or a feast— whether it is to be made for man, or man is to be made for it:—whether, with the modern Pharisees, it is to be kept like Ash Wednesday and Good Friday, or, with Bishop Cranmer, Edward the Sixth, Elizabeth, and all our early reformers, it is to be kept like Easter Sunday and Christmas-day; and it may be added also, with all

---

*Strain not your scythe, suppressors of our vice,
Reforming saints! too delicately nice!
By whose decrees, our sinful souls to save,
No Sunday tankards foam, no barbers shave:
And beer undrawn and beards unmown display
Your holy reverence for the Sabbath-day.
BYRON, *English Bards and Scotch Reviewers.*

the Catholic and Greek Christians, and many of the
followers of Luther and Calvin, at Geneva, and several
parts of Germany, beyond all comparison much the
greater part of the Christian world.

76. If it were observed to our little, though increasing
junto of Puritans, that it is incumbent upon them to pay
some attention to the great majority of the Christian
world, who entertain an opinion on this subject different
from them, and that they ought not to be too confident
in their own judgment, but to recollect that it does not
become them in fact, though perhaps not in name, to
assume to themselves that infallibility which they deny
to the united church of Christ with the Pope at its head;
they would probably reply, that they have a right to
judge for themselves, that they will not be controlled
by Antichrist, or the scarlet whore of Babylon. With
persons who can make this answer, the author declines
all discussion; he writes not for them, but for persons
who, having understandings, make use of them : and to
these persons he observes, that he does not wish their
opinions to be controlled by any authority; but he begs
them to recollect the beautiful story of the cameleon —
that others can see as well as themselves; and that when
a great majority of the Christian world is against them,
it is possible that they may be in error; and that therefore it is incumbent upon them to free their minds from
passion or prejudice as much as possible, in the consideration of this very important subject. That on the decision respecting it depends the question, whether the
Christian religion is to be a system of cheerfulness, of

happiness, and of joy, or of weeping, wailing and gnashing of teeth.

77. It is unnecessary to add any thing more upon this subject. It has been shown, that the intention of the writer of the first chapter of Genesis, and of the remainder of the Pentateuch was, to teach that the institution of the Sabbath was expressly limited to the children of Israel ; that it was a sign of the covenant betwixt them and God ; and that the sign and the covenant went together. It has been shown, that it was abolished by Jesus, when he did not enumerate the Sabbath amongst the commandments which he ordered to be retained, and by his conduct in breaking it on various occasions. It has been shown, that it was abolished at the first council of the Church, held by the Apostles at Jerusalem ; and that St. Paul has in the clearest terms, and repeatedly, expressed his disapprobation, not only of Sabbaths, but of the *compulsory* keeping of set-days as an ordinance of religion. Not a single passage can be produced from the Gospels or Epistles, in approbation of the continuation of the Sabbath, or of the substitution of any day in its place. Nor can it be shown, that the early Christians considered the observance of Sunday as the renewal of the Jewish Sabbath, or in any sense as an institution of divine appointment ; and therefore, from a careful consideration of the whole argument, and of all the circumstances relating to it — its antiquity — its utility when not abused — and the many comforts which it is calculated to produce to the poor and working-classes of mankind, it may be concluded, that the observance of Sunday

is a wise and benevolent *human*, but not *divine* ordinance ; a festival, which it is on every account proper and expedient to support, in such due bounds as will make it most conducive to the welfare of society. That with Christians it ought not to be a day of penance and humiliation, but of happiness, joy, and thanksgiving, as it was established by Edward the Sixth at the Reformation ; a festival, to celebrate the glorious resurrection of their Saviour to life and immortality.

WHEN THOU PRAYEST, ENTER INTO THY CLOSET : AND WHEN THOU HAST SHUT THY DOOR, PRAY TO THY FATHER WHICH IS IN SECRET ; AND THY FATHER, WHICH SEEST IN SECRET, SHALL REWARD THEE OPENLY.*

---

* One of the quotations from the Gospel of Luke is not taken from the orthodox version. The author being in the habit of consulting different versions, copied it from the wrong version by mistake, and did not discover it till the sheet was printed off. It is of no consequence whatever to the argument: and he only notes it that he may not give a handle to ill temper, to accuse him of misquotation.

FINIS.

The Liberal Classics, (No. 1.)

History of Christianity

Comprising all that relates to the Christian religion in " *The History of the Decline and Fall of the Roman Empire*," and, also,

⊁A VINDICATION⊱
(never before published in this country,)

of "SOME PASSAGES IN THE FIFTEENTH AND SIXTEENTH CHAPTERS," by

EDWARD GIBBON, Esq.

With a Preface, Life of the Author, and Notes by PETER ECKLER; also, Variorum Notes by GUIZOT, WENCK, MILMAN, "an ENGLISH CHURCHMAN," and other scholars.

One vol., Post 8vo, 864 pages, with Portrait of Gibbon and numerous Engravings of mythological divinities. Ex. vellum cloth, $2.00; half calf, $4.00.

" This important work contains Gibbon's complete *Theological* writings, separate from his historical and miscellaneous works, showing *when, where,* and *how* christianity originated ; *who* were its founders ; and *what* were the sentiments, character, manners. numbers and condition of the primitive Christians. What has been said by Christians in regard to the *Origin of Christianity* is reprinted from the valuable notes of Dean Milman, Wenck, Guizot, and other eminent Christian historians who have edited Gibbon's works : and the pious but scholarly remarks of the learned editor of BOHN's edition of *Gibbon* are also given in full. Among the numerous illustrations will be found representations of the principal divinities of the Pagan mythology The sketch of the author's life adds value and interest to the book, which is not only well edited and printed, but substantially bound. It will be a treasure for all libraries." — *The Magazine of American History.*

The Liberal Classics, (No. 2.)

Voltaire's Romances.

A New Edition, Profusely Illustrated.

"I choose that a story should be founded on probability, and not always resemble a dream. I desire to find nothing in it trivial or extravagant; and I desire above all, that under the appearance of fable, there may appear some latent truth, obvious to the discerning eye, though it escape the observation of the vulgar." — *Voltaire.*

CONTENTS.

THE WHITE BULL; a Satirical Romance.
ZADIG; OR FATE. An Oriental History.
THE SAGE AND THE ATHEIST.
THE PRINCESS OF BABYLON.
THE MAN OF FORTY CROWNS.
THE HURON; OR PUPIL OF NATURE.
MICROMEGAS. A satire on mankind.
THE WORLD AS IT GOES.
THE BLACK AND THE WHITE.
MEMNON THE PHILOSOPHER.
ANDRE DES TOUCHES AT SIAM.

BABABEC.
THE STUDY OF NATURE.
A CONVERSATION WITH A CHINESE.
PLATO'S DREAM
A PLEASURE IN HAVING NO PLEASURE.
AN ADVENTURE IN INDIA.
JEANNOT AND COLIN.
TRAVELS OF SCARMENTADO.
THE GOOD BRAMIN.
THE TWO COMFORTERS.
ANCIENT FAITH AND FABLE.

One vol., post 8vo, 480 pages, with Portrait and 82 Illustrations.   Paper, $1.00; Extra vellum cloth, $1.50; half calf, $4.00.

Voltaire's satire was as keen and fine pointed as a rapier.—*Magazine of Am. History.*
A delightful reproduction, unique and refreshing. — *Boston Commonwealth.*

Christian Paradoxes.

The Characters of a Believing Christian in Paradoxes and Seeming Contradictions.

BY

FRANCIS BACON, (LORD VERULAM.)

10 pages, post 8vo, with portrait. Paper cover, 10 cents.

From the doubts these *Paradoxes* imply, it seems reasonable to suppose that Bacon was of those who believe that religion should be taught in a symbolical and mystical language that the initiated and learned few may understand, and the great multitude believe ; and also that its true meaning should be veiled and hidden in paradoxes and parables, "that seeing they may see and not perceiv' and hearing they may hear and not understand."—*Preface*.

A NEW EDITION, JUST PUBLISHED, OF

VOLNEY'S RUINS

AND

THE LAW OF NATURE,

TO WHICH IS ADDED

VOLNEY'S ANSWER TO DR. PRIESTLY, A BIOGRAPHICAL NOTICE
BY COUNT DARU, AND THE ZODIACAL SIGNS AND
CONSTELLATIONS BY THE EDITOR ;

Also, a Map of the Astrological Heaven of the Ancients.

Printed on heavy paper, from new plates, in large clear type, with portrait and illus.
trations. One vol., post 8vo, 248 pages ; Paper, 50c. ; cloth, 75c. ; half-calf, $3 oo.

This is undoubtedly one of the best and most useful books ever published. It eloquently
advocates the best interests of mankind, and clearly points out the sources of human ignorance and misery. The author is supposed to meet in the ruins of Palmyra an apparition or
phantom, which explains the true principles of society, and the causes of both the pros-
perity and the ruin of ancient states. A general assembly of the nations is at length
convened, a legislative body formed, the source and origin of religion, of government,
and of laws discussed, and the Law of Nature—founded on justice and equity — is finally
proclaimed to an expectant world.

"VOLNEY'S *Ruins* will be read with as much interest to-day as it was a hundred years ago.
It is a book that was born to immortality and a hundred years to come it will be as fresh as
it is to-day"—*Religio-Philosophical Journal.*

The Liberal Classics, (No. 5.)

Superstition in all Ages

OR, "LE BON SENS,"

✛ By JEAN MESLIER, ✛

A ROMAN CATHOLIC PRIEST,

Who, after a pastoral service of thirty years in France, wholly abjured religious dogmas, and asked God's pardon for having taught the Christian religion. He left this volume as his last Will and Testament to his parishioners and to the world.

TRANSLATED FROM THE FRENCH ORIGINAL BY

MISS ANNA KNOOP.

Post 8vo, 339 pages, with Portrait. Paper, 50 cts.; cloth, $1.00; half calf, $3.00. The same work in German. Cloth, $1.00.

The work of the honest pastor is the most curious and the most powerful thing of the kind that the last century produced. . . Paine and Voltaire had reserves, but Jean Meslier had none. He keeps nothing back; and yet, after all, the wonder is not that there should have been one priest who left that testimony at his death, but that all priests do not.—*James Parton.*

THE SOCIAL CONTRACT,

Or *PRINCIPLES OF POLITICAL LAW.*

Also, A PROJECT FOR A PERPETUAL PEACE,

BY

JEAN JACQUES ROUSSEAU, *Citizen of Geneva.*

One volume, post 8vo, 238 pages, with portrait, extra vellum cloth, 75c., paper 50c.

The writings of Rousseau, says Thomas Paine, in his *Rights of Man*, contain "a loveliness of sentiment in favor of Liberty that excites respect and elevates the human faculties."

"He was the most directly revolutionary of all the speculative precursors. His writings produced that glow of enthusiastic feeling in France, which led to the all-important assistance rendered by that country to the American colonists in a struggle so momentous for mankind. It was from his writings that the Americans took *the ideas and the phrases of their great Charter.* It was his work more than that of any other one man, that France arose from the deadly decay which laid hold of her whole social and political system, and found that irresistible energy which warded off dissolution within, and partition from without."—JOHN MORLEY.

"He could be cooped up in garrets, laughed at as a maniac, left to starve like a wild beast in a cage,—but he could not be hindered from setting the world on fire.—THOMAS CARLYLE.

PROFESSION OF FAITH of the Vicar of Savoy,

BY JEAN JACQUES ROUSSEAU,

Also, A SEARCH FOR TRUTH, by Olive Schreiner.

Post 8vo, 128 pages, with portrait,   Vellum Cloth 50c., paper 25c.

The Liberal Classics, (No. 7.)

THE WORKS OF THOMAS PAINE.

Life of Thomas Paine, by Editor of the National with Preface and Notes by Peter Eckler. Illustrated with views of the Old Paine Homestead and Paine Monument, at New Rochelle, also, portraits of Thomas Clio Rickman, Joel Barlow, Mary Wollstonecraft, Madame Roland, Condorcet, Brissot, and the most prominent of Paine's friends in Europe and America. Paper 50 cts.: clo .75

The Age of Reason ; being an investigation of True and Fabulous Theology. A new and complete edition, from new plates and new type ; 186 pages, post 8vo. Paper 25 cts. ; cloth 50 cts.

Common Sense. A Revolutionary pamphlet, addressed to the inhabitants of America in 1776, With an explanatory notice by an English author. Paper 15 cts.

The Crisis and Common Sense. The *Crisis*, written in " the times that tried men's souls " during the American Revolution, was preceded by the revolutionary pamphlet *Common Sense*, which awakened the desire for freedom and independence. 300 pages, post 8vo. Paper 30 cents, cloth 50 cents.

The Rights of Man. Parts I and II. Being an answer to Mr. Burke's attack upon the French Revolution. Post 8vo., 279 pages. Paper 30 cts., cloth, 50 cts.

Paine's Complete Theological Works.—Age of Reason, Examination of the Prophecies, etc. Illus. edition. Post 8vo, 432 pp.; paper 50 cts.; cloth $1.00·

Paine's Political Works.—Common Sense, The Crisis, Rights of Man, etc. Illustrated edition. Post 8vo, 650 pages ; cloth $1.00

Paine's Great Works. Popular edition. 1 vol. cloth, $3.00.

FORCE AND MATTER

OR

Principles of the Natural Order of the Universe,

WITH A SYSTEM OF MORALITY BASED THEREON.

BY

PROF. LUDWIG BÜCHNER, M. D.

A scientific and rationalistic work of great merit and ability. Translated from the 15th German Edition, revised and enlarged by the author, and reprinted from the fourth English edition.

One volume, post 8vo, 414 pages, with portrait, vellum cloth, $1.50; half calf, $3.00.

CONTENTS:

Force and Matter,
Immortality of Matter,
Immortality of Force,
Infinity of Matter,
Value of Matter,
Motion, Form,
Immutability of Natural Laws,
Universality of Natural Laws,

The Heavens,
Periods of the Creation the Earth,
Original Generation,
Secular Generation,
The Fitness of Things in Nature, (Teleology),
Man,
Brain and Mind,
Thought,

Consciousness,
Seat of the Soul,
Innate Ideas,
The Idea of God,
Personal Continuance,
Vital Force,
The Soul of Brutes,
Free Will,
Morality,
Concluding Observations.

Rob't G. Ingersoll's Writings.

ONLY AUTHORIZED EDITIONS.

Ingersoll's Lectures Complete. In One Volume: Half Morocco, Containing over 1,300 pages. Price, $5.00.

Prose Poems and Selections. In silk cloth, $2.50; in half calf, $4.50; in full Turkey morocco, gilt, $7.50; in full tree calf, $9.00.

The Gods and Other Lectures. Comprising The Gods, Humboldt, Thomas Paine, Individuality, Heretics and Heresies. Paper 50c.; cloth, $1.

The Ghosts and Other Lectures. Including Liberty of Man, Woman, and Child. The Declaration of Independence, About Farming in Illinois, Speech Nominating James G. Blaine for Presidency in 1876, The Grant Banquet, A Tribute to Rev. Alex. Clarke, The Past Rises Before Me Like a Dream, and A Tribute to Ebon O. Ingersoll. Paper, 50c.; cloth, $1.

Some Mistakes of Moses. Contents: Some Mistakes of Moses, Free Schools, The Politicians, Man and Woman, The Pentatench, Monday, Tuesday, Wednesday, Thursday, He Made the Stars Also, Friday, Saturday, Let Us Make Man, Sunday, The Necessity for a Good Memory, The Garden, The Fall, Dampness, Bacchus and Babel, Faith in Filth, The Hebrews, The Plagues, The Flight, Confess and Avoid; Inspired Slavery, Marriage, War, Religious Liberty; Conclusion. Paper, 50c.; cloth, $1.

Interviews on Talmage. Being Six Interviews with the Famous Orator on Six Sermons by the Rev. T. DeWitt Talmage, of Brooklyn. to which is added a Talmagian Catechism. Paper, 50c.; cloth, $1.25.

Ingersoll Field Discussion. Faith or Agnosticism. Discussion between R. G. Ingersoll and H. M. Field, D. D. Paper, 50c.

Blasphemy. Argument by R. G. Ingersoll in the Trial of C. B. Reynolds. at Morristown, N. J. Paper, 25c.; cloth, 50c.

What Must We Do To Be Saved ? Analyzes the so-called gospels of Matthew, Mark, Luke, and John, and devotes a chapter each to the Catholics, Episcopalians, Methodists, Presbyterians, Evangelical Alliance, and answers the question of the Christians as to what he proposes instead of Christianity, the religion sword and of flame. Paper, 25 cents.

A VISIT TO CEYLON

BY

ERNEST HAECKEL,

PROFESSOR IN THE UNIVERSITY OF JENA. AUTHOR OF "THE HISTORY OF CREATION,"
"HISTORY OF THE EVOLUTION OF MAN," ETC.

WITH PORTRAIT, AND MAP OF INDIA AND CEYLON.

TRANSLATED BY CLARA BELL.

One volume, post 8vo, 348 pages, extra vellum cloth, $1.00.

———

Before venturing on this memorable voyage to India and Ceylon, whose results have delighted and entranced many readers in both hemispheres, our enthusiastic author, having conferred many zoological titles in honor of the august divinity that controls and governs the solar orb, claimed in return special consideration and protection from the occult forces of that brilliant luminary, and hoping to be favored with pleasant and agreeable weather during the entire voyage, he made, with all the solemnity that becomes a scientist, the following propitiatory invocation to *Helios*, the benignant god of the Sun:

"I beseech thee, adored Sun-god, that this, my zoological tribute, may find favor in thine eyes! Guide me, safe and sound, to India, that I may labor in thy light, and return home under thy protection in the spring."—*Haeckel's Visit to Ceylon, page 20.*

"These letters constitute one of the most charming books of travel ever published, quite worthy of being placed by the side of Darwin's '*Voyage of the Beagle.*'"—*Nation.*